Corpus Christi Writers 2023

Edited
By

William Mays

Copyright

For more information contact
William Mays
Mays Publishing.
Books@mayspublishing.com

Cover Design by Alexis Mays Harborth

Copy Editor Tom Murphy

Special Thanks to Joseph Wilson

Printed in the United States of America

ISBN
9781733469654

Introduction

The *Corpus Christi Writers* series strives to present diverse views and perspectives that, taken as a whole, reflect what people in South and Central Texas are thinking. Many writers from previous anthologies return to this sixth book in the series, and many new writers join them. Youthful exuberance coexists with polished style. The themes vary and express the unique viewpoints of the writers.

Cursive writing makes a comeback in this volume, and a 1952 Royal Quiet Deluxe Typewriter makes a guest appearance. Submissions about ranching, fishing, and the roaring waters of the Gulf of Mexico provide a strong sense of place. Compelling female voices speak out about spousal abuse, violence directed at women, and a desire for identity outside traditional male-defined roles.

We provide a forum for all forms of writing from what might be considered "traditional" to what might be called "post-modern" or "experimental" or "visual poetry." As part of our goal to develop unique expression, we feature the work of local artists and photographers who view familiar landscapes from a slightly different perspective. While the print version is black and white, full color versions are available in the Kindle version along with bonus content.

Biographies tend to be shortened in the book. For full bios and bonus content, please go to https://mayspublishing.com/. The site is updated daily and receives robust traffic. It includes links to writers' websites. On MaysPublishing.com, we welcome writers from anywhere in the world and rotate their work through our social media promotions.

First Lines by William Mays

Table of Contents

Introduction 3
First Lines 4
Table of Contents 5
Alamgir Hashmi 9
Alan Berecka 10
Alice Marks 12
Alisa Hope Wagner 14
Albert Morales 15
Ricardo Ruiz 18
Alyanna Mena 19
John Morris 20
Alyson Greene 22
Cynthia Giery 24
Alyssa Outhwaite 25
Lu Ann Kingsbury 28
Carol Mays 29
Mandy Ashcraft 31
Christian Garduno 32
Charles Etheridge 35
Claire Taylor 38
Jeff Janko 39
Clara Isabel Tamez 40
Cynthia Breeding 42
Jeff Janko 45
Dennis Denman 46
Devorah Fox 49
Donna Huddleston 52
D. Weiss 54
Tom Murphy 56
Dragon Bodhing 57
Dylan Lopez 58
Elizabeth N. Flores 60

Ellissa Brewster 62
Esther Bonilla Read 64
F.E.I. 66
Gerald Beckman 69
Jacob R. Benavides 71
Jacqueline Gonzalez 72
J. L. Wright 73
JoAnn Sanderson 74
Nicole Serrao 77
Joel Ortiz 78
Joseph Wilson 80
William Mays 83
Judy Bloomquist 84
Jill Scott 86
Judy Mastenbrook 87
William Mays 88
Karen Cline-Tardiff 89
Sister Lou Ella Hickman 90
Jeff Janko 92
John Meza 93
Juan Manuel Perez 96
John Pettigrove 99
John Morris/Michelle Zudrell 101
Julieta Corpus 104
Kimberly Ward 106
Lizbette Ocasio-Russe 107
Louise Knolle Pettigrove 108
Lucas Jasso 112
Mason Graves 114
Matthew Rosas 115
Michael Quintana 117
Michelle Eccellente Stevenson 118
Mike Mercer 120
Jeff Janko 122

Mona Schroeder 123
Jen Deselms 125
Neesy Tompkins 126
William Mays 128
Neina Chapa 129
Lu Ann Kingsbury 131
Octavio Quintanilla 132
Pete Adler 134
Pete Lutz 135
Roberta Dohse 138
Robin Carstensen 141
Roy Gomez 144
Sarah K. Lenz 148
Scott Wayland Griffin 150
Margaret Cleaves 154
Sophia Chapa 155
Cynthia Giery 156
Stephen Gambill 157
Kerstin Berger 158
Susan Daubenspeck 159
Tito Perez 160
Tom Murphy 163
Tonāntzin Rodríguez 166
Wayne Hankins 169
William Mays 170
William Walton 172
Sarah K. Lenz 176

Alamgir Hashmi

Alamgir Hashmi is the author of numerous books of poetry and literary criticism. He has taught as a university professor and is Founding President of The Literature Podium: An Independent Society for Literature and the Arts. In the mid-1970s, he read some of his poems in Corpus Christi on a panel with local poets. He notes, "My morning and evening shoreline walks in the area were a special pleasure for me, with only an occasional *norther* keeping me indoors at my desk or chatting with friends."

Now and Then

Window-pane shatters too noisily
for the heart when
silently a word cuts through
and cancels a probable simile.

Meanwhile, we tuck ourselves together
in midst of passion when
suddenly the door knocks
and we think, "it's just bad weather!"

At times, speech is referential
that explains much less when
urgently it should do more
and prove that a soft kiss is essential.

So our days pass into the ideas we live
which makes them our betters when
normally we should pass away
and no more think we can take and give.

Alan Berecka

Alan Berecka was the poet laureate of Corpus Christi from 2017-2019. He is the author of five books of poetry, and his work has appeared in numerous journals and websites. He earned his living for many years as a librarian at Del Mar College in Corpus Christi. In January 2023, he finally lived long enough to put down the date due stamp and retire.

Total Immersion

For Richard Whatley

My friend Richard, now in his 80's
finally retired from his furniture store.
A Baptist to the core he called me
late on a weekday night, stone sober,
auditioning, if you will, to be a character
in some future poem that I "should" write.

He reminded me of the time a gale force
gust of wind caught my pushcart
on the 8th hole, how it picked up speed
all on its own, how it flew like Evel Knievel
did in Vegas, that time Evel jumped
the fountain at Caesars Palace,
but the unmanned cart once launched
flew more like a wounded duck with my wallet
and cell phone riding in the attached bag
how it splashed down in the pond's middle,
and how I had to jump in and wade out
into the chest high gunk before it sunk,
and then soaking wet and barefoot missed
my short birdie putt, how I went home
mad, sad and sodden, and if that one
won't do maybe I could write about the time
on the same hole, how our friend Boyd
who is a mountain of a man tried to hit
his ball out of the water at the pond's edge
and ended up looking like the Swamp Thing.

Richard says he's sure these poems
would be hits. I tell him I have my doubts,

but Richard reminds me he's a can-do-
kind of guy and says all he can do is try.
I pass on the crack about him being trying,
stunned by how much the entry
into literary obscurity means to him.

I await his next call.

Alice Marks

While she lives in Duluth, Minnesota, Alice Marks has written a series of mysteries entitled *The Corpus Christi Mysteries*. This story is based on *RV Murders*, the final book in the series.

Murder at Richland RV Park

You've probably heard the horrific news. It's all over the TV. Last night a murder befell the tranquil haven for compatible senior citizens, Richland Villa RV Park, Corpus Christi. I'm unable to share any details because I don't know a thing about it. I'm just another resident.

Police officers swarmed the Park. This incident has undermined the sense of security we residents have always enjoyed. From chatter I heard in the Community Center, most agree it had to be an outsider. Others, who are afraid a killer dwells among us, want to leave right now. Hot-shot detective Stan Belkin, who just arrived, says no one can leave until we have all been interviewed because we are all under suspicion. Can you believe that? One of us kind, friendly, law-abiding seniors is a murderer? No way.

One resident said he doesn't give a rat's ass what the detective said, he and his wife are leaving. Roxanne, the usually easy-going, jolly owner who appears on the brink of a break-down, urged the couple to stay. The next day we learned he and his wife sneaked away during the night. They gave the guard some sob story, and the dimwit let them go. Detective Belkin is having kittens, and the last thing we need around here are more cats. Roxanne has a passion for them, and they are everywhere. Ha! Ha! That was a good one! Belkin says security will be increased. The police have put out an APB with description of the couple and their rig.

Calm resumed here for a couple months. Most of the Winter Texans have left as they usually do long before summer with just a few staying to support Roxanne, poor gal. Stan Belkin and his partner, the cutie Maria Gonzales, have gotten nowhere solving the murder. That isn't because they haven't had suspects, two of them, believe it or not, both residents. One was a reclusive guy who lives here year-round, and none of us know him. He had an alibi and several witnesses. At the time of the murder, he was stuck in traffic because of a pile-up on SPID, right before the causeway. The other is Dick Morten, Saintly Dick as we call him, the least likely resident to be guilty of any crime. The detective ruled him out, of course. Now this is pure gossip, but via the grapevine I've heard the two detectives may be paying more attention to each other than the case!

The only thing I know for certain is it's one hot summer. The T.V. meteorologists attempt to outdo each other in describing the heat and humidity as sweltering, like smelt burning, scorching, intense, searing, broiling, and melting. In addition, the slightest hint of a tropical in the Atlantic has the public buying up plywood to cover windows as hurricane preparation.

Chaos ensued at Richland today. The runaway couple drove back in a brand-new tricked out Luxury model RV! At the same time, a uniformed cop was in the process of arresting Dick Morten when Belkin appeared, screaming the cop was an imposter arresting an innocent man. The detective hit the fake cop so hard that he fell down the steps from the RV. Belkin jumped on top of him and pummeled him. Petite Maria, who doesn't look like she could subdue an angry canary, pulled Belkin off the fake police officer before there was a second RV Park murder.

With her partner suspended—and not getting in her way— Maria found another resident she believed suspicious, and she discovered "solid" evidence in his RV. Personally I find this ludicrous. Not him! He's really a great guy and we couldn't be closer. I'll find the best defense attorney in Corpus.

It's November now and the so-called RV murderer is on trial. The defense lawyer I found has done everything to discredit the evidence. I keep hoping the judge will toss it out. He doesn't. The Prosecution is elated. This isn't right.

The trial has dragged on for days, but now it's with the jury. Hours pass until the bailiff calls everyone back to the courtroom. The foreman reads the verdict: Guilty of murder in the first degree.

A few weeks later The RV Murderer, a Richland resident, receives his sentence. I'm on my way to Huntsville Prison.

Alisa Hope Wagner

Alisa Hope Wagner is an award-winning author, editor and publisher of over 30 books. She married her high school sweetheart, and together they raise their three children in a Christ-centered home.

A Writer's Toil
Illustration by Albert Morales

His hands shook. Where was his brandy? He patted his trousers. Nothing. He had been just about to take a drink. The air suddenly lacked life. The atmosphere chilled his skin. A dream. Or maybe another hallucination. He tried to stand up, but his feet were fastened to the chair.

"My cousin! Have you locked me up again?" he shouted.

"Your cousin, you say? Tell me about her," a woman's voice chimed.

He didn't recognize the accent. "Who are you? Where am I? Why Can't I see?"

"You are still in Virginia. We must keep the room dark to minimize visual stimuli. I just have a couple of questions for you. It won't take long. Then we will bring you back to what you were doing before. What were you doing?"

"I was drinking my damned brandy!" he yelled. "Why can't I stand?"

"You must stay seated if you want to go back," the voice sounded. "Were you in your aunt's home?"

"I demand an explanation! I will not answer any further questions!"

"That's too bad. You will not remember any of our conversation. It will be disappointing to go through all this work and not get to know you a little more."

"Why would anyone want to know me?"

The voice paused. Her breath vibrated like tinkling bells. A chair scraped against the concrete floor, and her rapid breathing drew closer.

"They required that I not say anything except ask my questions to verify the facts. I was hoping this day would come; and when it did, they requested the expert. Me."

"Expert of what?"

"You, of course."

"Me!"

"How about this?" she dinged. "We will have a question-and-answer game. I will answer one of your questions and you will answer one

of mine."

He brushed his arm across his parched mouth. He wished he would have taken his second drink of brandy. "I'm first. Where am I?"

"You are in Virginia."

"That is not what I meant!"

"Well, you are the writer, aren't you? Ask more specifically. My turn. What have you written so far?"

"How do you know I'm a writer?" he inquired.

"If you are not going to play this game correctly, we will not play."

"Only two books of poetry. They did poorly. I'm surprised you know them."

"I know much more than that," she clinked a laugh.

He thought. "What exactly does this facility do?"

"We take famous people for brief moments to verify facts. What writing are you working on currently?"

"I don't know," he answered.

"Impossible!" the voice rang out. "You, the literary genius, have nothing? That is not an answer!"

He held up his hands. "No, it is true. I never know until it knocks into me. Then I must scribble as fast as my hands allow. It is like trying to capture a fading vision before it vanishes."

"Very interesting!" the women's voice pealed.

He thought. "How is it that you know more about me than I do?"

"Now that is a question from the master! I know everything about you because I've spent my life studying you. When this vision comes to you, is it fully complete like a gift of words?"

He shook his head. "No, I gain only a feeling.... a mere glimpse that I must wrestle to reveal. It can take days or weeks to grasp the entirety of it. It is quite laborious."

"How wonderful," she jingled.

"Does everyone know my work?" he asked.

"Everyone that matters. We teach you. We study you. Your writings changed literature, as we know it! And I should know. I am the expert."

"Yes, so you have mentioned."

"Your struggle with words is what makes your life and writing so very intriguing. Your angst is something we no longer experience. Our lives are quite boring and easy now," her voice resonated.

"Easy," he rasped.

A bell sounded. "Oh no!" the woman's voice tolled. "You are about to be sent back. I am not supposed to do this, but please, give me your signature on this page."

"What is it?" he asked.

"It is your life's work," she dinged melodiously. Her breath tickled his mustache. She placed the book on his lap. "Here, take my pen and sign it quickly before you leave."

He placed his hand on the book feeling its thickness. His life's work. Done. No wrestling. No striving. Given freely without the fight. A life of both renown and ease. He scribbled his signature and held up the pen. "A pen, you say. I like it."

"Regrettably, you must give it back. They say if you bring anything back from our time, it will trigger your memories."

"I will give it to you." He clenched the pen with his fist and stabbed it into the breath of the voice, silencing the infuriating cadence as sweet sounds of moaning and groaning choked it out.

He dropped the pen and clutched the book in his desperate arms.

His eyes opened. His tumbler stumbled across the wooden floor, spilling the brandy. Was it another cruel dream? Had fate tricked him again? He loosened the grasp of one hand and pounded his chest twice. *Thump. Thump.* A book, indeed. A book! A large volume of his own work! He gripped the volume with trembling fingers and brought it to view. He beamed over the hardcover like a father over his newborn son and gently wiped the splattered blood with his sleeve. "The Complete Works of Edgar Allan Poe," he whispered in awe. "I am a writer who will never have to wrestle words again."

The full color version of this 6 1/2 foot by 36 foot mural by Ricardo Ruiz was commissioned by Reforma, a nightclub/restaurant, in Palm Springs CA. Check it out the next time you're in Cali

Alyanna Mena

Some live to work; Alyanna works to live. She lives in Corpus Christi.

Figment

The heart monitor sped then slowed as the doctor pushed what consisted of liquid milk into my vein

Knowing that I missed breakfast

And as foggy as winter glass, did my vision fade into a lucid hibernation

The scalpel served the first glass of wine, then the second.

A knight sat at the round table, with a full course and I am but a pawn. But in that moment, I felt like the queen.

My lipstick stained the polished armor as it dazzled in the light that hung above the island. The music carried us to the sofa where the real game was about to begin.

That familiar hazy feeling came back and settled as my body started to radiate warmth. My cheeks flushed matching the scarlet that I had placed on my lips.

I thought carefully about my movements on the checkered board but it seemed I was one step behind his. In this dance we mirrored our steps, yet I was stuck looking down trying not to trip from the exhilarating intoxication.

He brought my face to his and smiled.

Checkmate

The saline dripped steadily as the fluorescent light shook me awake. And in that moment I wanted to go back.

John Morris

Padre Island

John Morris

A Sense of Desperation

My morning started out differently as this small boat built by hand and fueled by desperation washed in with the tides as I watched. It had been marked OK, visible on all sides and from above…a postscript that there was now no one aboard…hopefully they were rescued or made it safely ashore somewhere.

Alyson Greene

Alyson Greene facilitates a weekly writers' support group and book club via zoom through The Writers' Studio of Corpus Christi. She is happiest when playing in the waves with her husband and children.

Firsts

I didn't want to go out on the water. Seth, Amber, and I had spent our childhoods running along the soft sand and splashing in the warm surf. But we weren't kids anymore and Amber had moved away. In the weeks since she'd left, I saw everything in the sharp contrast of before and after. I didn't know how to be the same girl without her.

But when Seth flashed a dimpled grin asked me to go kayaking, I thought maybe we could find a way to bridge the gap between the kids we were and whatever we were becoming.

We didn't speak as we paddled away from where his dad had beached the boat. The wind worked against us, but even without words, we soon became synchronized and both did two strokes on the right for every one on the left.

Once we were around the bend of the weed-covered shoal, I felt Seth stop paddling behind me. I stopped too and balanced the paddle across my knees. Droplets of water dripped down my legs.

"I'm sorry," Seth said.

"For what?" I tried to turn to look at him, but the kayak wobbled too much.

"I don't know. Are you mad at me?"

"No. I miss Amber," I said.

"Yeah." Seth cleared his throat and swirled his finger through the water beside us. "I mean, it was just practice, right? It didn't mean anything."

The night before Amber moved away, she'd explained how she couldn't start ninth grade without knowing how to kiss. The three of us had shared so many firsts together, and she'd said she couldn't imagine having a first kiss with anyone else. Hope had bloomed in my chest at her words, but as I watched Amber's lips meet Seth's, it curdled in my stomach. They'd pulled away, giggled, and kissed again. I'd run out of the room, nauseous.

"Were you jealous?" he asked.

"No," I lied.

"Everything's fine, then?" He sounded skeptical.

"Yup."

He slapped the surface of the water, splashing me. Despite its warmth, my spine tightened at the shock of it. I let out a laugh.

"Come on, talk to me," he whined. "Amber's gone and I can't..."

His voice trailed off, but I knew what he meant because I felt it too. In one night, I'd lost them both.

I was too scared to look at him, but I'd never held back from him before.

I gathered my courage and passed my paddle back to Seth. "Hold this." I inched my body around to face him. The kayak rocked as I moved but Seth shifted his weight to counterbalance mine.

"Have you ever kissed anyone?" he asked.

"No. You know I haven't."

He shrugged as if I could have a harem of lovers he didn't know about. "Have you thought about kissing anyone?"

I scoffed. "Of course! Loads of people."

"Oh, okay." His dark brows lifted above his sunglasses. "Could I see this list?"

"What list?"

"Of the people you want to kiss." He made small splashes in the green water.

I felt my lips twitch up in an uncontrollable grin. "Why do you want to know?"

He splashed me again. "You know."

I laughed and splashed him back. "Say it!"

He leaned over to fling more handfuls of water at me. The kayak rocked. We stopped splashing and steadied ourselves. Seth shifted his weight. "Can I kiss you?"

I took a steadying breath. "Everything's changing."

"That isn't a bad thing." His face softened.

I leaned toward him, placing a hand on his shoulder. I stopped with my face centimeters from his and whispered, "Don't let me fall in."

"Never," he whispered back.

I kissed him. His mouth was warm and salty like the gulf. The buckles of our life jackets clicked against each other. The kayak swayed. We pulled apart.

"See?" he smiled, like everything had been fixed.

Except it hadn't, because I wished his lips were Amber's.

Cynthia Giery

Corpus Christi Skyline on a Foggy Day

Alyssa Outhwaite

Alyssa is a graduate student at Texas A&M University- Corpus Christi, who enjoys writing poems and stories whenever she gets the chance. She loves creating pieces that can be interpreted many ways depending on the reader's feelings and background.

Fuzzy Perspective

10 March,
Today was it. The day I called it quits. I gave up entirely. I couldn't take it anymore. I was a kettle, screaming for attention, but no one came to remove me from the heat. My water has evaporated. Hot metal and remnant condensation is all that is left of me.

12 March,
I've spent all weekend in bed. Even now, my blankets lay bunched around me. A testament to the poor sleep I've gotten. Did I eat recently? I can't remember; I'm not hungry. I should probably have some water, but the kitchen is so far away. Down the stairs. My legs are weak. Better to stay here.

13 March,
I continue to wake and sleep. All around me feels so disorienting. Am I alive? I can't be certain. I hear them talking on the phone again. He's worried about me. Murmurs of 'depression.' I wish I could muster the energy to care. They don't understand. All hope is gone. Nothing has ever hurt me this much.

15 March,
"Sweetie? Are you okay?"
I feign sleep. Nothing matters anyways.
His sigh is deep, but he strokes my head, leaving a gentle kiss behind. It makes me feel a little better, I guess.
"You hungry?"
No. Not today.
He leaves me be. It's for the best.

18 March,
"Baby, come on. You need to get up."
I can't help my sigh. I hate this. I hate being pestered.
I want to scream at him, 'NO, leave me be.'

Instead, I roll over, ignoring his commands.
"Seriously? Why are you acting like this?"
I resist the urge to snap back at him.
"Please? At least come with me outside for a bit?"
I can tell he's trying so hard.
He's hurting too.
I give in this time.
The sun might feel nice.

23 March,
"I don't know what to do. She hardly leaves the bed."
He's on the phone again. I don't know why he acts like I can't hear him.
I came to the living room like he wanted!
We were watching TV, not that I was really paying attention.
"Yeah, I know. This is just getting out of hand."
I'm offended, I came down here for him.
Angry, I leave the couch to go back to the bedroom.
Life is stupid.

30 March,
Time always passes weirdly, but it's especially slow lately. Days feel like months. Or years. I don't know. He tries to comfort me. Sometimes it works, makes me oddly content? Just the feeling of his hands wrapped around, hugging me softly.
It's nice.
But it's not his arms I want.
He knows it too.
I hate hurting him.

1 April,
I'm staring at the door again.
It's become a habit.
It's dumb because I know nothing is going to change.
She's not coming back. No matter how much I want her to walk through those doors again.
It's hopeless to think otherwise.

5 April,
"I'm home!"
That voice?
Can it be?
No. I can't get my hopes up.
But I'm already down the stairs, heart pounding.
And there she is.

Eyes bright, hair a wild mess of waves.
Everything falls back into place again.
He's there, kissing her, hugging her.
Bastard loves to make me jealous.
I don't wait now.
I go to her.
She lowers to the ground, her knees at my feet.
"Did you miss me sweetie?"
As her arms wrap around me, the world feels right again.
I lean into her with all my weight, making her laugh.
"I told you she's been depressed since you left."
"Aww. She loves her mommy. My good girl."
Yes.
I am a good girl.

Lu Ann Kingsbury

Sand and Sky

Carol Mays

Carol Mays wrote three books about talking cats: *Nevins*, *Nevins 2*, and *Mortimer*. She also wrote *103 Crazy Ideas for Surviving Suburbia.* With her husband, William, she wrote *Escape from Sunny Shores.* She and her husband manage Mays Publishing.

Rise Up Fight Back

Oh, hey! Hi! You're back! Have a seat. I like sitting on the porch, don't you? The weather is so nice this time of year. The last time we visited I was telling you all about my trailer.

I've discovered something completely sinister. I don't know why I did *not* notice it before. I mean it was right in front of me all the time. Come to think of it everywhere in front of me: the news, social media, even when I am in public. I need to start at the beginning because it's spreading like a mind-controlling virus.

Oh, you have that look on your face! No! don't go! Here, have some of your favorite wine. Just sit a minute and listen.

It all started a few years ago when I decided to talk to a neighbor I would see every day on my walk. Most of the time I would just smile and wave hello. It's the suburban thing everybody does. It's so fake, but it's the norm. I knew her because her kid and mine had a class together many years ago. We began to walk and talk about blah, blah, boring blah stuff. Nothing out of the ordinary. Just a couple of housewives who gave up a career to raise a family. She shared how she had joined her husband's religion, which was mine too, so we had that to talk about. I was and still am less religious than her, but I gave her a pass because I thought she was just some enthusiastic—albeit annoying—convert. Whatever. She would go on and on about church stuff. Then, one day she seemed different. Still goody-goody, but on steroids. She was more nervous than normal. More fearful. It was this day—I am sure of it that I realized something sinister was going on not just in the neighborhood, but in the world, too.

I won't tell you the full details of what she told me, because I'm not one to gossip. Suffice it to say that she told me about something her husband wanted, and she wasn't comfortable with his suggestion. So, he's a bit of a freak in bed, but it really wasn't that bad. In my mind all she had to do was say no—which she did, but then, she felt she was in a true dilemma. *This* is where it gets weird. She robotically blurts out, "I must obey my husband." I started laughing. I mean, she's got to be kidding me. Right?! This has got to be a joke. This woman had a major career. Massive education in an Ivy league school, came from a wealthy family and she has to do what?! Obey?! What are we in the 1800's? I thought she was joking, but she wasn't! It was like that movie, The Stepford Wives. She started quoting Bible scriptures. Get real. We're Catholics! I don't remember any Bible stuff. I mean stories, yeah, but not like nut-job stuff. This was like a cult-level, Kool-Aid drinking moment. She went on to say that she wanted to do anything to please her husband. *ANYTHING!* So, she took this and other succeeding problems to the *priest! She had him on speed dial! Seriously?!* As time progressed, it became obvious she couldn't do anything on her own. At first, I tried to encourage her to be creative. A kind of female empowerment. When that failed, I had to ask why. She said her biggest fear was her husband divorcing her which would mean she would not have her suburban lifestyle. I told her that if I were her, I would help him pack, get half of everything and move on. Oh, here. Your're empty. Have some more wine. This is where it gets *really* good.

I tried to make agreements with other wives, simple stuff like garbage can and brush placement between our properties. If their husbands didn't agree, then all our days of negotiations went down the tubes. These men act like kings and these annoying wives act like servants or more accurately robots. It didn't stop there. If the husbands noticed that their wives were developing friendships with other women then, they would interfere. As a result, their wives would break off all communication immediately. Why? They fear loss of their status or worse, harm to their children even if the kids were adults in college. It always boiled down to the husbands controlling the finances. The wives do all the work in the house and care for the kids, even the adult ones while the husbands get all that free time to further develop their careers. Then, when the husbands finally die and let's face it, they die first, social security cuts off the checks until the death certificate of these rotten men is registered leaving the women to fend for themselves with no prior warning that this financial cut-off was going to happen! This brings me to right now. *Huh!*

All over the world women are suffering from the moment they are born. I thought at first it was just my area or neighborhood. No. In the name of religion, and it doesn't matter what religion, women are suppressed. We are held back. Our bodies are not our own. Men infiltrate every single aspect of a society worldwide and use force to make us suffer. Then, use women to subjugate other women. It's sick! That's why we need to rise up and fight back! We need to get an awareness group together. We could use my trailer for meetings and start out small with four of us, because that's all my trailer can seat. We could call our group the "R.U.F. B's pronounced *ruf-b's* for Rise Up Fight Back. Get it? What do you think?

Wait. Did I hear you correctly? You *have to ask your husband* before you can join the group?!

Mandy Ashcraft

Self-portrait
In celebration of
National Women's Day

Christian Garduno

Christian's work can be read in over one hundred literary magazines. He lives and writes along the South Texas Coast with his wonderful wife, Nahemie, young son, Dylan.

Montana Jake v1

Clenching his teeth
Montana Jake took an uppercut swing
and nailed The Trapper squarely
The Preacher tried to intervene
as he believed in peace + love between his brethren
but The Preacher quickly jumped a few paces back
when he saw the look in Montana Jake's eyes--
it was a look of altogether rage splashed with
a helping of righteousness
The Preacher duly departed with the words:
See y'all on Sunday!!

Irritated, Montana Jake continued with a solid
left cross and when The Trapper whimpered
Montana Jake knew that it was all over
not one to kick someone when he knew they were beat
Montana Jake spat on the ground and said without disgust
yet more matter of factly: I knew you was a tramp thief!!
The Trapper knew the beaver colonies well enough
and some say he got what he deserved
others said they wouldn't want to be around when
The Trapper came for his revenge
still others said he should have just finished off The Trapper

That evening by his fire
Montana Jake realized how close he was to being overcome
by the poison vehemence that swells up in his fists
he thought to himself that he was lucky
he didn't have to face The Judge today
or pick up his pack and make a run for it again

Montana Jake wasn’t sure how many more fresh starts he had in him
One thing was certain
he would have to stay up til dawn
just to make sure The Trapper didn’t try anything clever
Montana Jake sharpened his axe thinking things over in his mind

After a long while without making a sound
Montana Jake decided he would get himself a dog
or rather, a puppy
that way he could train it to swim and catch fish
Montana Jake knew a Ute woman who could find him the right one
and figured he could barter a few beaver skins and a pouch of tobacco
Her name was Birdwhistle
she kept many animals and knew the names of all the trees in the land
when Montana Jake was bitten by a snake last autumn
Birdwhistle nursed him and soothed the bite with her own saliva
he made up his mind right then he would name the pup Birdy in her honor

Cabrillo & 27th

Landlines + expired bus transfers
was it 19th that went though the park?
we'd walk over from The Richmond to The Sunset
over to Leonski's and knock
oh nobody's home
well, hell, turn around and walk back the hour walk back thru the park in the dark
where T Styles is laying down beats
and a war has started in a far far away galaxy
well, as long as they don't blame me

I used to work with Hippie Gram -not Punk Rocker Gram-
I had to be there 3 AM Ferry Plaza Bldg
that's when we had to start the fire on Saturdays
and we couldn't use lighter fluid
so we used apple chips and newspaper and also lit cigs off that
by five am, it was roaring and we cooked until we sold out of meat
well, we gave away more than we cooked
and if I'm honest, I think Hippie Gram traded even more away
he got shit in return

It was called ██████ FAMILY FARMS
and they was fam
the ranch was up by Mount Shasta
I never went but I know Hippie Gram did
they both made a lot of money from each other
Hippie Gram used to crack the fortune cookie
take out the fortune and read the fortune
sigh and throw away the cookie
then he'd chew the fortune

Charles Etheridge

Self-proclaimed desert rat Chuck Etheridge was raised in El Paso, Texas. He served in the navy and worked as an actor, a convenience store clerk, a Rent-a-Poet, and a catalog copy writer before finding employment as an English teacher.

How Shakespeare Saved the Earth

I am a female Norwegian elkhound named Shakespeare. On March 19, 2014, I saved Earth from invasion by the planet Xgorpia. A housewife, a boy, and a garage door opener helped.

It was a normal morning. My humans had locked me in the garage to protect me from Animal Control. Their concern was nice, but my ancestors nipped at the heels of charging elks. Evading dog catchers isn't a challenge.

My garage door opened. I saw six tall men in matching outfits at my neighbors' open door.

Jimmy, my friend, stood on the porch.

"Jimmy," I barked cheerfully. "What's going on?" All humans hear is "Bark, bark, bark." I liked Jimmy.

One man swung around, drawing a squirtgun. "What did you say?"

"I was asking Jimmy," I began... "Wait a minute. You understood me?"

"Yes. Our translation software doesn't seem to work on humans."

I trotted closer. Something was off. Each man looked identical and had pointed ears.

Something familiar…

"Why do you all look like Leonard Nimoy?" I asked.

"Hi, Shakespeare," said Billy. "These men knocked but I can't understand…."

"Who's Leonard Nimoy?" asked the closest Nimoy.

"An actor on a Sixties TV show my human watches."

"All humans look alike to us. We wanted to blend in, so we reviewed communications from your military organization Desilu Studios and chose a typical human appearance."

"Desilu Studios? A military organization? Leonard Nimoy? A typical human!" I laughed.

"Why is Shakespeare barking now?" Linda, Jimmy's mom, appeared at the door.

"You're revealing operational secrets," hissed another Nimoy.

"This species forces humans to talk, Leader. I apologize."

Leader Nimoy said, "Our scouting reports didn't fully assess the threat. Neutralize it."

"Threat?" I asked.

Nimoy raised his squirtgun and fired.

Garage doors all over the neighborhood closed.

"What was that?" I asked.

Both Nimoys looked terrified. "It's immune to advanced weaponry!"

"Jimmy," said Linda. "Take Shakespeare home. Gentlemen, come inside." Linda's gracious.

She calls me "dog" and pretends she doesn't like me, but she sneaks me treats. Classy lady.

He grabbed my collar and put me in my yard.

"Sorry, girl. Gotta follow the Law of Mom." He petted me. "I'll come back after these weirdos leave. We'll play."

"Okay," I said. He heard "Bark."

I waited, ran, and leapt over the gate.

The neighbors' front window was open. Linda served each Nimoy lemonade. All six held glasses, none drank. What do they think? She's going to poison them? Jimmy took a big gulp of lemonade.

Then the other Nimoys felt safe. Most took a slug, looked at each other, surprised, then chugged, emptying their glasses. One sipped and put the glass down. The other five gestured for more.

"Well," said Linda, "I can't understand a word y'all say, but you sure like lemonade."

Something's off. One Nimoy slipped off his chair. Another stared at his hand. Another turned to the Nimoy next to him and said, "I know this is bad timing, but I have feelings for you."

"Mom," said Jimmy. "They're acting drunk."

"Is the lemonade too tart?" she asked the nearest Nimoy.

That Nimoy stared longingly, saying, "You have the most beautiful knuckles I have ever seen."

"Thanks?" Linda said.

I'd had enough. I scrambled through the open window and barked, "You leave her alone. She's Jimmy's mom."

The Nimoy who had only one lemonade sip produced his squirtgun and fired.

Every radio in the house started playing "Tequila." (Yes, I know my Fifties music. Blame my human.)

Amorous Nimoy grabbed Linda's hand and blew lustily on her knuckles. Linda jerked away.

"You B movie wannabees better leave now," I barked.

"But we must contact humans," said Sober Nimoy, "And blend into their society."

I growled.

Amorous Nimoy grabbed Linda's hand again and tried to lick her knuckles. I nipped his heels like he was an elk in Norway.

He yipped and backed away, terrified. I lunged at another Nimoy, snapping my teeth. I wasn't gonna bite, but they didn't know that. I lunged and spouted old movie lines like "Do you feel lucky?" and "If I want your opinion, I'll beat it out of you."

I backed them to the door Jimmy had opened. Once the Nimoys were outside, Jimmy slammed the door.

Out on the front lawn, I charged at Sober Nimoy and barked, "Tell me what's going on right now." I also needed them out of sight. The garage. I thought. "Shoot me again," I told Sober Nimoy.

Terrified, he raised the squirtgun at me and fired.

The neighborhood garage doors opened.

"In here." I herded them into the garage—being a herding dog comes in handy when corralling six Leonard Nimoys.

Once inside, I told Sober Nimoy, "Shoot again." The garage door closed.

Trying to growl menacingly, I questioned Sober Nimoy. "Who are you? Why are you here?"

"We are from Xgorpia. We are a peaceful people, but your military agency called Desilu Studios began transmitting messages about coded operations in which your ships travelled the galaxy forcing planets to join something called the "United Fred-rated of Something."

"That doesn't make sense," I said.

"Yes, I now realize Desilu Studios was a ruse concealing the fact that you are this planet's dominant species." He looked worried.

Me? Dominant? I realized he meant dogs. "Uh, yes. We are in charge. And clever. And very angry about being invaded."

Nimoy said, "It was a terrible mistake. Release us, and Xgorpia will never bother Earth again."

I growled and negotiated more to make sure they were good and terrified. Eventually I let them go. Sober Nimoy called his starship for a rescue. A UPS truck appeared on the driveway and honked.

The driver looked like Leonard Nimoy.

Later, I was making my rounds—remember, no fence can hold a Norwegian elkhound. Linda and Joe called me over. Joey fed me a Milk Bone and Linda scratched me behind the ears, cooing, "Who's a good girl?"

And that's how I, Shakespeare, saved the earth.

Claire Taylor

Claire Taylor graduated from Magnolia High School in 2023. She has been writing and recording songs since she was fourteen.

Out Of Tune Piano

It's an out of tune piano, but I'll still press the keys
Playing broken melodies with empty memories.
It's an out of tune piano, singing tiredly
Trying hard to just keep up with my new modern beat.

So, when I find I'm shattered, and lying on the ground
Even if I'm battered, I'll still come around
Then I'll hit that note and find
I still feel like I can fly
Singing each note perfectly
Even on an out of tune piano.

It's an out of tune piano, but it still stands tall
Making shattered harmonies to play in a new song.
It's an out of tune piano on it's final leg
The symphonies that we have shared, the bonds of two best friends

So when I find I'm shattered, and lying on the ground
Even if I'm battered, I'll still come around
Then I'll hit that note and find
I still feel like I can fly
Singing each note perfectly
Even on an out of tune piano.

No one made a piece on an out of tune piano
Learn not to fear the price of doing something wrong
Cause true beauty will last long
True beauty will last long.

So when I find I'm shattered, and lying on the ground
Even if I'm battered, I'll still come around
Then I'll hit that note and find
I still feel like I can fly
Singing each note perfectly
Even on an out of tune piano

Jeff Janko

Statue in the Cemetery

Clara Isabel Tamez

Clara Tamez was born in Corpus Christi. She holds a Bachelor of Arts degree from the University of the Incarnate Word in English and a Master of Fine Arts degree in Creative Writing from Kingston University London. She currently resides in San Antonio.

Margaret

"That's nasty," Margaret said. She had just returned from the showers. She dumped her pajamas and toothbrush on her cot and knelt beside me. "Where is it?"

On the underside of my left arm right above my armpit, what could easily be mistaken for a squirming speck of dirt, was a lone star tick. Two months ago, I would've gagged at the sight of this thing with legs burrowing its head inside me, but it was the last day before summer camp ended and I just wanted this one off.

"Jenna, can you hand me the first aid kit?" I asked while experimenting with which ways I could hold my arm without squishing the bug or pushing it in further.

"Sure. You won't find tweezers in there though." Jenna shrugged her vest on. "The older girls took them all this morning. Something about doing their eyebrows now so the redness fades away by tonight."

I rolled my eyes. On the last night, there was always a big dance across the lake. The Boy Scout camp was dirty and the boys there, arrogant. I didn't understand the overwhelming need to gush or imagine romantic scenarios about them like the older girls did. When they came over for archery practice every Wednesday, they laughed and slapped each other on the arm when girl after girl missed. They were silent when we didn't.

"Do you want me to dig through their stuff?" Margaret asked, already jumping up. "I bet Christina knows where they are."

"No, I guess we can just find Liz."

Jenna held the tent flap open for us and I hopped off the wooden platform first. There weren't that many mosquitoes, I remember that distinctly. Usually, they climbed all over us but that morning they didn't bother.

The three of us linked arms and walked into the forest, kicking stones as we went. At the fork in the road, Jenna went left, toward our morning class of Arts and Crafts, and Margaret and I went right. She held my hand as we passed the bathrooms and talked about how they're probably located that far in the woods to air out all the smell because think about it, have you ever *seen* anyone clean it? That made me wrinkle my nose. We wound through the trails to the mess hall, the route memorized. If we took a right by the v-shaped tree and continued straight, we would end up by the Trail Stop by the camp entrance. But if we took a left there instead, down that thin, dusty path, it would turn into a longer, sweatier hike to the other side of camp: a hill with looming archery targets.

We were told to always look out for landmarks, so we chose a clump of what looked like poison ivy but wasn't–they're not the only leaves of three–next to the bush that on the second week of camp we hid behind wearing white sheets before jumping out and scaring Jenna. That mark, where Jenna jumped and we screamed in laughter, is how we knew we were on the right track.

The smell of fresh javelina poop struck us when we rounded the final bend, warm and stinging. Margaret already whipped out her survival kit, as Liz and the rest of the counselors called it; though I questioned how, if it came to it, we could survive off a whistle, flashlight, a multipurpose tool, and poop bags. I held my nose as she tried to pluck it off the trail.

"Ugh, what did that one eat?" I pretended to gag but it really did smell bad.

Although it smeared and smelled worse when she touched it, she scooped with confidence.

"Children's hopes and dreams, probably." She grinned and grabbed my hand again, the bag swinging in her other.

The only other thing we saw on the trail was a forgotten hair tie. I picked it up and handed it to Margaret. She placed it on her wrist like a bracelet.

After all, Girl Scouts always leave a place better than they find it.

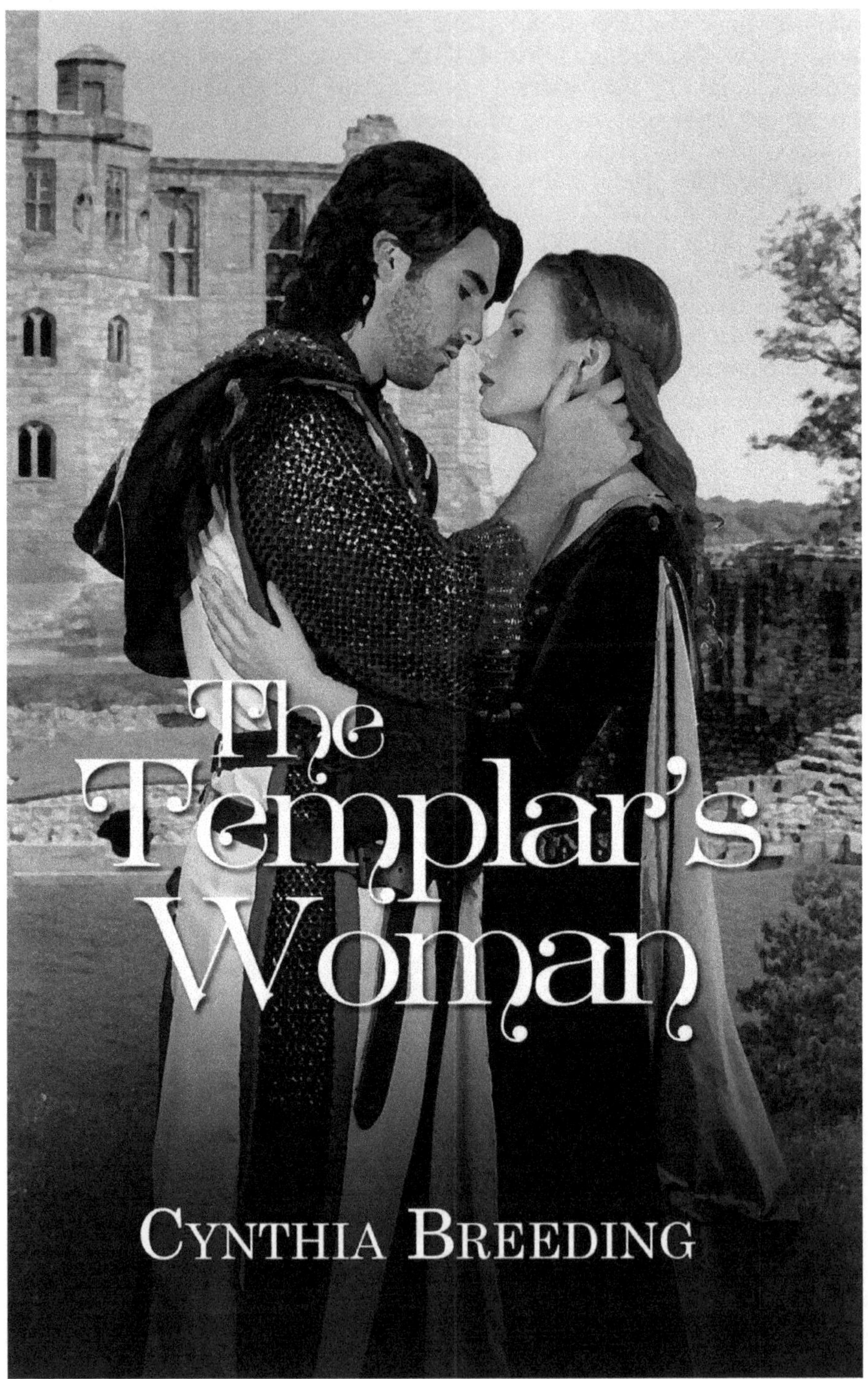
The Templar's Woman
Cynthia Breeding

Cynthia Breeding

Cynthia Breeding is a well-established romance writer with over fifty novels and novellas. Most are available from traditional publishers.

Excerpt from *The Templar's Woman*

Prologue

October, 1307

Like ghostly wraiths, twelve ships glided silently around the headland of Orkney under the cover of night, tendrils of fog curling around the hulls and obscuring the sound of oars dipping into the flat water. A new moon shed only a sliver of light from its crescent as Adrian de Soules lifted his eyeglass to peer at the closing shore.

"Is the earl waiting, Captain?" Pierre Robillard, his first mate, came to stand beside him on the bow of the flagship.

"Not yet," Adrian answered, lowering his scope.

"He may not have seen our lantern with this thick mist." Pierre swiped at his face. "And it's *cold.* I'm going to miss the south of France."

"Better be cold and alive than dead," Adrian replied. "We were lucky to have enough warning to load the treasure before the king's men found it."

"Or us."

"*Oui.*" A muscle clenched in Adrian's jaw. "I just wish we could have gotten Jacques out too."

Pierre grimaced. "You know de Moray would never leave until the last Templar was safe."

Adrian knew that only too well. He'd spent several hours arguing with the Grand Master while the ships were being loaded. Word had been sent to his brethren scattered across France that Pope Clement—the damn fool puppet of King Philippe—had declared all Templars heretics and ordered them to be rounded up. It was only a ploy so the French king wouldn't have to pay the vast debt he owed to them, but they didn't have the numbers to launch a revolt against the entire French army, to say nothing of the Holy Roman Empire.

"I think I see something!"

Adrian raised his eyeglass again. Faintly, he saw a lantern swing in a half arch and then another a small distance from the first. "That's our signal. The entrance to the cove." He lowered the glass. "Give the helmsman the order."

As Pierre hurried away, Adrian turned his thoughts to Jacques once more. The Grand Master stayed because no Templar left his brothers on the battlefield to die. But de Moray was also right that the treasure the original nine men had recovered from the Temple of Solomon nearly two hundred years before had to be protected from falling into the greedy king's hands. Or worse, the Catholic church. The scrolls themselves would be enough to turn Christianity upside down, to say nothing of the ancient relics. Especially one relic.

He looked to the shoreline where he could now make out a half dozen men waiting with a couple of wagons. He had to have faith that Henri St. Clair, the Earl of Orkney and Baron of Roslin, had chosen trustworthy men for this mission, but *faith* was not one of Adrian's strong suits. He preferred dealing with physical things he could see, touch, and feel.

"Heave ho!" one of the sailors called out as several lines uncoiled like snakes and slithered through the air.

The men waiting on shore caught them and Adrian could feel the hull scrape against the sand as the boat was pulled forward. Waiting for the gangplank to be lowered, he wondered which man was Henri St. Clair, since they were all working to secure the ships and no one was standing about like a grand lord. A good thing, in Adrian's estimation. The earl was also a direct descendent of the St. Clair family whose daughter the first Templar, Hugh de Payen's, had married, so he simply was the best choice to guard the treasure.

Besides, the Scots were in the middle of rebellion against the English. *That* was something Adrian could understand.

And the Templars could help.

Jeff Janko

Sunglasses

Dennis Denman

Dennis Denman grew up in a rural setting in the Calallen/Annaville area of Corpus Christi. He has been a veterinarian in the Corpus Christi area since 1974.

Heart of the Rancher

I drove west through the small towns of Banquete and Agua Dulce and turned on a Farm-to-Market road and drove another four or five miles. I passed the shop and farm house and turned into the entrance to the ranch headquarters on the opposite side of the road. I drove over the cattle guard, through the front pasture with the windmill, over another cattle guard past a hay lot, and over two low water crossings on the creek and then over another cattle guard. On my right were the cattle pens and to my left the office and ranch house. I went into the office and visited with the rancher for a few minutes, and then he got into his pickup and I got into my van to go check the cow.

I followed the rancher's pickup as we drove back to the front pasture and then turned off the caliche road and went to the far north end of the pasture. Not too far from the fence on the north side of the pasture lay the heifer I was to examine. The rancher pulled up about thirty feet from her. I stopped my van, and we both got out. The heifer had difficulty calving a month earlier and had damaged the nerves to her rear legs in the process. She had the calf on her own, but could not get up after calving due to the nerve damage. We had examined the heifer after she calved and given appropriate medications to see if she would recover from the nerve damage. The ranch hands had even built a shelter out of T-posts, cattle panels, and tarps to protect her from bad weather, but they had moved her out of the shelter since the weather had been nice for several days. They had fed and watered her daily and moved her and cleaned around her when they checked on her every day.

I got a few instruments from the back of my van, approached the cow, did a general physical exam, and then did a short neurological exam to determine the extent of the damage to the rear legs of the heifer. I was facing the heifer and my back was toward the vehicles and the rancher. As I stood back up from my squatting position, I heard the rancher speak from behind me. "She'll never get up will she, Doc"? I turned to face him and said, "No she won't".

While I had been examining the heifer, the rancher had gotten a five gallon plastic bucket out of the back of his truck. He had turned it upside-down on the ground, next to his truck, and was sitting on it when he asked me the question. After I answered he motioned me toward his truck and said, "Doc, get a bucket out of the truck and sit down here next to me."

We sat there on the buckets for three or four minutes before either one of us spoke. We were just looking at the heifer with our backs to the pickup. While we watched she made two or three attempts to get up, but her rear legs simply did not work. She was a Brahman-cross heifer between two and a half and three years of age.

"Look at her Doc, she's so beautiful".

"Yes she is".

"And look at her, she tries so hard".

"No doubt about that. Look how she gets up on her knees in the front, but her rear legs just won't work at all. And she is so feminine too."

"She is so feminine, she's beautiful, and she tries so hard. But she'll never get up will she Doc"?

"No. She will never get up. She is totally paralyzed in the rear legs."

We sat there on the buckets in silence for two or three minutes, and the rancher said, "I guess we need to do what we have to. We need to put her down."

It was not unusual, at the time, for ranchers to kill a cow with a gunshot to end their suffering when there was no chance of recovery. Properly placed, a gunshot is quick and humane. We were still sitting on the buckets looking at the heifer. "You know Doc, I have a gun in my truck and I know it is fast and humane, but you have some medicine you can use too."

"Yes I do, but it is more expensive."

"How much is it Doc?"

At the time the medicine would be about fifty dollars. I told the rancher how much it would cost and he didn't hesitate. "You know, Doc, a lot of people would say I'm crazy because I have a gun in my truck, and a bullet is a lot cheaper, and people think you don't get attached to cows. But she is so beautiful, and she tries so hard, and her being paralyzed isn't her fault."

"No it's not her fault; it isn't anyone's fault. It is just something that sometimes happens. You have done everything you can to see if she would recover."

"Well, like I said, Doc, people will think I'm crazy, but she is so beautiful, and she tries so hard. She deserves better than a bullet. You give her the shot to put her to sleep."

I went to my van, pulled the medication up in a syringe and walked back to the heifer. I slipped the needle into her vein, as the rancher held her head to one side with a rope, and gave the medication. The heifer relaxed, the rancher pulled the rope off her head and he turned to walk away as I listened with a stethoscope to be sure her heart had stopped. As I stood up from the heifer's side, I turned and the rancher was sitting back on one of the buckets beside the truck. I put the syringe and stethoscope back in my van and then went back and sat on the other bucket. We sat there, in silence, for a few minutes and then got up and put the buckets back in his truck. We shook hands and then got in our vehicles and drove away. Neither of us had spoken since he told me to give her the injection and I'm not sure either one of us could have. As I drove out of the pasture in my van, I realized I had truly seen into the heart of the rancher, and the tears which had accumulated during the few minutes of silence spilled out of my eyes and down my cheeks. I knew the same thing was happening in the truck ahead of me as we drove through the pasture toward the road.

Devorah Fox

Devorah Fox writes Fantasy/Science Fiction and Mystery/Thriller novels and short stories for adult and young adult readers. Find her work in paperback and digital editions on Amazon, Kindle Vella, Nook, and Kobo, and as audiobooks on Google Play Books.

Excerpt from
Drowning in Desire

CHAPTER ONE

I am fine. Maybe even a little excited. Yes, though I am afraid, I am also curious about what lies ahead. There will be doubt, there will be pain, I know. Reluctance, resistance, even rebellion. I expect that. One does not seek to conquer so potent a force as desire without a struggle. Desire is a cruel master that in ruling my life has ruined my life, forcing me to do things and make choices that led me away from perfect peace. But conquer it I will. I must, if I am to live. Here in this cell, devoid of distractions of any kind, I will wrestle with desire, until one of us emerges the victor.

Though I am naked I am not cold. The room is at a temperate constant. Though there are no lamps, it is not completely dark. A sliver of light from the corridor glows in the crack between the floor and the door, which is locked from the outside. With this light, I can assess my surroundings. They are as I requested: bare. There is nothing on the smooth, matte, bone-colored walls. No furniture, so I sit on the floor. The pale vinyl tile is hard and unyielding under my bones, and clammy. It does not absorb my perspiration. But this is a minor discomfort.

***

Though I am tired of sitting, I resist the urge to stand. Yes, I am stiff, numb, my back aches, my legs have gone to sleep, but I don't really need to stand, I simply want to. This is what I am here to fight.

Hunger is not a problem, although I have been fasting for days to purge my system in preparation for this battle. Within mere hours of starting the fast, I began to plan what I would eat when I emerged victorious. My fantasies ranged from the simple pleasure of toasty chestnut-and-citrus-scented hot tea with lemon to the decadence of savory steak and tart beer, so vivid I could feel the hot juices and cold bubbles on my tongue. But I recognized these for what they were, pure cravings, not a genuine need for nourishment. I am in no danger of starving to death.

Thirst is another matter. A man can go only about three days without water before dehydration becomes life-threatening and this may be a long siege. So I have water, a small glass, only four ounces, but it would be enough to restore my strength, save my life if it comes to that. It is up to me, however, to save my soul.

***

I am thirsty, have been for some time. Time? How much time have I been here? Unable to determine the passage of time by the corridor light which never dims or brightens, I have tried to tell time by counting my breath but now time has become meaningless, the measuring of it absurd. I have been here as long as I have been here.

Thirst is a constant now. It varies in degrees of intensity from mild and manageable, like a dull headache, to torturous, a demand that clamors to be satisfied and won't be ignored. I try to turn my attention away by focusing on something else.

I count the floor tiles. This room is six by nine.

I count the white acoustical ceiling tiles. There are six complete tiles and three partial tiles. There are holes in the tiles and I count them also. I don't count the number of holes in one tile and multiply, I count each individual hole. Altogether there are 7,590 holes in the ceiling tiles. And I do not drink.

***

The size of the room, the concept of time, the length and depth of my breath pale in significance to the materiality of my thirst. The only thing more real is the glass of water. My vision is blurred and I can no longer see the room clearly but I can see the glass.

I can imagine how the water tastes without drinking it, can feel the cool, satin smoothness of the glass against my lip, feel the fluid moisten and cool the inside of my mouth. I can taste the salts and minerals, the chlorine and the fluorine . . . still, I do not drink.

***

All this imagining has done nothing to decrease my desire for water, desire accompanied by pain so severe it has a life of its own, ebbing and flowing, now here in my throat, now there in my stomach. I cannot ignore it, don't have the energy to rise above it.

Pain is my existence. Pain, breathing, and the glass of water. A generous quart, there is enough to have a sip now and still have some for later when I'll need it. But if there will be a later when I will need it more, then I do not need it now, I only want it. I will not drink.

***

I am beyond thirsty; I am desiccated throughout. My skin is dry and tight, cracked, my tongue shriveled and my body has shrunk in on itself. I am so dizzy I can hardly stay conscious let alone think, so weak I cannot move even to shift off a pebble digging painfully into my side. Surely no one human has gone this long without water and survived.

The walls are indistinct as though they were miles away and though I am lying on the floor I cannot bring it into focus. I can only see the glass of water. It is a huge glass cistern the size of a corn silo, sixty feet tall and thirty feet wide. Down one side sluices a single drop, as big as my head.

I stand poised on the rim of the glass, look down into its clear depths. I dive in. My skin plumps as parched cells soak up the moisture. Bathed in cool water, my organs cease to grind hotly, painfully against each other and function was a well-oiled machine. My heart beats with renewed vigor and my blood, no longer thick as sludge, once again flows in my veins.

Deeper and deeper I dive, drinking as I go. I can't get enough fast enough. I drink my way to the bottom of the cistern and lie there swollen like a water balloon. My lungs, starved for oxygen, urge me back up. I struggle to rise, but I have gone too deep and am too bloated. Why did I drink so much? I have learned nothing. I should have had just a taste, just one lifesaving sip instead of gorging myself.

The water is thick as gel. I flail my arms, kick my legs but they won't move. If only I could grasp the rim of the glass, I could pull myself up and out but it is just beyond reach. I stretch my arm out but the rim is too far away. I can't hold my breath any longer. My stomach, chest. and lungs expand. Water floods in.

Donna Huddleston

Dr. Donna Huddleston has a long history of service to the community as a public health nurse and as a home health and hospice administrator.

Customary Prayers for Marie

"I'm only thirty-four years old," Marie said. "I'm too young to die."

That morning, she ran away from her husband, ten-month-old daughter, and four-year-old son. She drove to an emergency room a hundred and fifty miles away, hoping for a different prognosis and then came back home.

I cleaned her bandaged arm, the familiar alcohol lingering from a pad placed by another nurse.

"The other nurse said the Pet Scan would hunt and illuminate my little cancer critters," Marie said between sobs. "They like sugar." Then she calmed. "Nurse, I need you to pray with me." She grabbed my hand. "There were too many of them little critters; I saw them glowing as they munched on me."

I wasn't used to praying; I never thought I would be asked to pray—chaplains did that—or nurses of a particular faith. I had heard the hospice chaplains tell patients and their families—*I will pray in the custom I'm used to if that is okay with you.* It usually was. As a Unitarian, I don't usually pray; we meditate, practice mindfulness, or visualize healing energy. I could see how this translated into prayer. *Amen, So Be It,* and *Namaste* were frequently heard in church after meditation.

Marie wasn't Unitarian; she was Catholic; she had prayer beads around her neck and her Blessed Scapular. She kept touching the beads with her slender fingers, but they did nothing to soothe her brow. I hooked up the oxygen concentrator, placed the cannula in her nares, and waited for her to relax. My interventions had little effect.

Prayers seemed like the only option. I did know that a lot of Catholic prayers were repeated over and over. I looked for a prayer book. She lacked one.

"How about the Lord's Prayer?" I asked. Even I knew that

one. I pulled a chair closer to the bed and sat down.

"No, I don't like that one."

"Then how about the twenty-third Psalm? I know that one by heart."

"No. I don't like that one either."

I racked my memory for a prayer. Finally, I said, "I know 'Now I Lay Me Down to Sleep.' When I was a child, my grandmother used to say the prayer with me when I stayed the night as I was afraid of the dark. Do you know that one?"

"Yes," she said, her bald head nodding up and down as she agreed. "That one will do."

I handed her a tissue, and she dried her eyes.

"Now I lay me down to sleep," I said, repeating a centuries-old prayer from the 1700s. "I pray the Lord my soul to keep."

"Yes, yes," she said. "That is the one."

Then the dark part, "If I should die before I wake, I pray the Lord my soul to take."

"Again," she said. I started over again, and she repeated it with me. We prayed the words at least thirty or forty times before she was fast asleep. Michael, her husband was in the kitchen; he had finished feeding the baby. He let me out the backdoor.

D. Weiss

D. Weiss is an English major at TAMU-CC. One of her favorite pastimes is playing D&D.

Excerpt from Scorned Raven Trials.

"Your marriage in the East will forge an iron clad alliance! You should see it for the great honor it is! Now, go!"

The words rattled around in Alessio's head like an agitated hive as his brow furrowed. Being the king of the Northern Realm, his father was used to telling and never asking what should be done. That attitude had doubled as of late. This time, Alessio was **told** that he was chosen by the princess of the largest kingdom in the East as her prospective husband. Aside from his father's haste, Alessio could not help but find something else odd about the whole situation. *"The old man is getting desperate, but why? And why did the princess request me specifically?"* he sighed. *"At the very least, maybe I'll be able to pay an old friend a visit."*

With how he weaved in and out of thought, the ride to the castle seemed to take both an eternity and only a moment. Brought back to reality by the sudden jostle of the carriage as it stopped, Alessio found himself at the grand structure's gates. Rumors about the castle at the base of Ila failed to do it justice. Many had remarked about the various flora that decorated the castle's landscape, a showcase of color at every turn. While it was busier than what he was used to, it also didn't feel like useless clutter. It just felt like...*life*. It also didn't escape his notice how tirelessly the servants were moving about the grounds. *"I suppose this uproar is because of the engagement*" he pondered. As he stepped out, one of the attendants gave him a smile before bowing deeply.

"Prince Alessio, welcome to Ila! My name is Donovan. We hope you enjoy your stay!"

"Thank you, the hospitality is very much appreciated. I'm looking forward to my time here" Alessio managed a polite smile.

"Very good sir, the royal family is happy to have you. We can start with a tour of the grounds" the other man enthusiastically stated.

"Actually, do you mind taking me to the princess? Since she requested my presence, I would like to give her my regards" the young man stated. While he'd rather not appear rude, Alessio was eager to speak with the princess. If not to get an explanation, at least to know more about his fiancé. *Fiancé.* That word didn't feel quite real to him yet.

"Yes sir, she should still be in her room. Follow me" the servant gestured. As they headed inside, Alessio scanned the marble halls. The castle seemed vast, halls stretching to multiple rooms filled with servants and a stairway framing the upper floor. It had been some time since his own home felt as vibrant as this. Before he knew it, they had reached the princess's room, marked by a door bearing an emerald.

"Your highness, Prince Alessio has arrived! He wishes to speak with you" Donovan stated.

A moment later, a young woman's voice called back. "Ah, wonderful! Come in!"

With a quick encouraging look from Donovan, Alessio took a breath before entering. As the door closed, he put on a smile, ready to give her a formal greeting. However, when the young woman turned to face him, his words immediately caught in his throat. Surprisingly, it was a familiar face that greeted him. Though, her attire differed vastly from their last encounter. Dirtied armor and boots traded for an emerald laced dress and heels. Once disheveled, curly, dark hair in a messy bun now neatly framed her shoulders with a tiara nestled on top.

"Nice to see you again, Alessio. How have you been?" she smiled.

It took the auburn-haired man a bit to respond, the vice-captain of the royal guard he once knew was...a princess?! "...Fleur...Wait a minute, you're the princess?! But you told me you were...!" he exclaimed.

"Heh, I know I have some explaining to do. And I promise I will in detail" she replied, giving him an apologetic smile. "...I'm just glad to see you."

Afterwards, Fleur wrapped her arms around Alessio in a gentle hug. Slowly lifting his arms to reciprocate it, he could feel that nagging sense of unease return. Though their prior time together had been short, the prince knew Fleur was not one to do things without good reason. Although, there was one question at the forefront of his mind.

"Fleur, all of this about our arranged marriage, is it true?" he gazed down.

Pulling away, Fleur gave a small sigh. "In a sense, yes, but not completely of my doing. I did request for you, but to receive you as an old friend. My parents, however, jumped at the chance to assign a suitor with promise. I'm sorry."

At that, the prince couldn't help but let out a chuckle. *"Of course, what other reason would there be? I should have known. No doubt my father's work as well"* he thought. "It's fine, thank you for explaining. But as for *your* reasoning, was it just for a friendly visit?"

Fleur's expression changed once more, a mix of hesitation, worry, and another unreadable emotion in her gold flecked eyes.

"No, that wasn't all. There is something more pressing. I've had dreams, or rather, visions of horrible things. A war, people screaming, our homes in flames, and—you. Different, changed somehow—and chained to the walls of the temple where we met."

Tom Murphy

Journal Entry

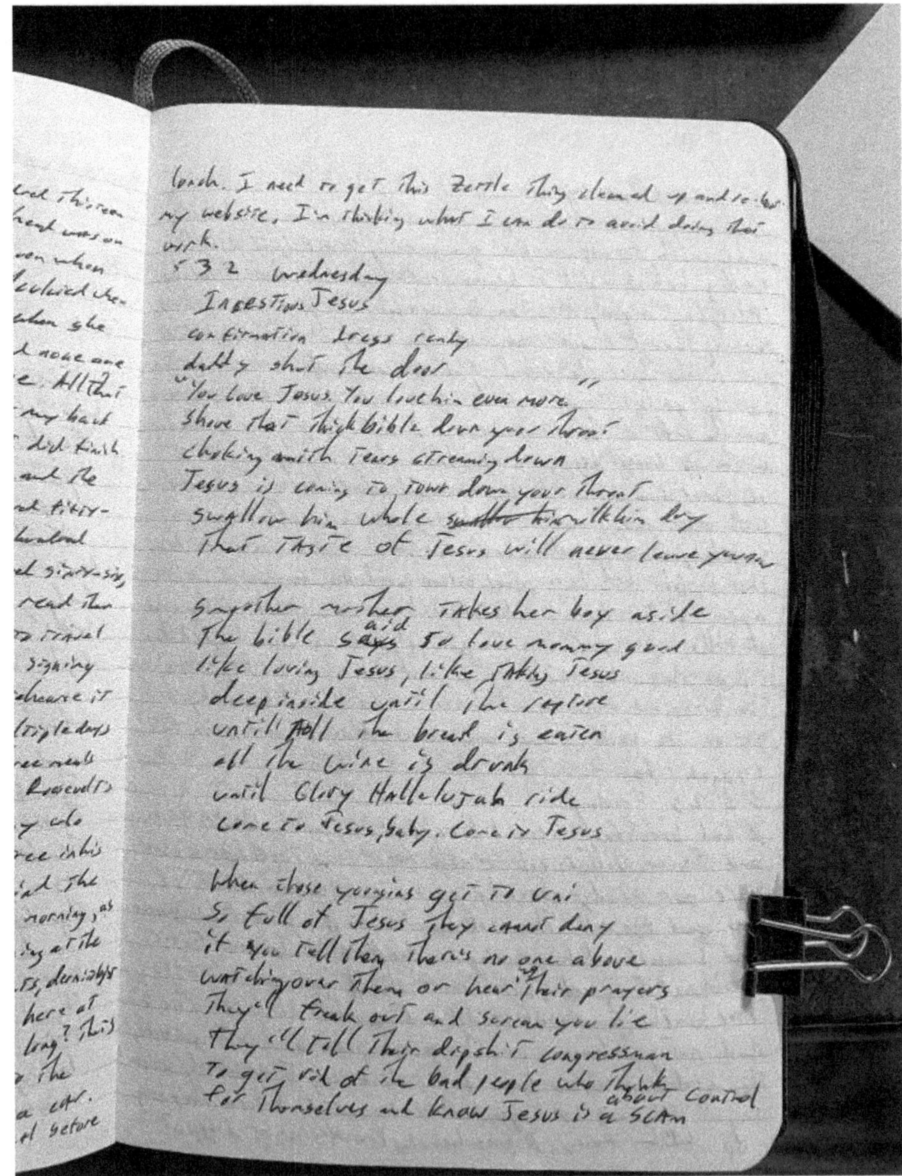

lunch. I need to get this Zettle thing cleaned up and re-do my website, I'm thinking what I can do to avoid doing that work.
5 3 2 wednesday
Ingesting Jesus
confirmation dress ready
daddy shut the door
"You love Jesus. You love him even more."
Shove that thick bible down your throat
choking with tears streaming down
Jesus is coming to town down your throat
swallow him whole until he's all the way
That taste of Jesus will never leave your mouth

Smother mother takes her boy aside
The bible said to love mommy good
like loving Jesus, like taking Jesus
deep inside until the rapture
until all the bread is eaten
all the wine is drunk
until Glory Hallelujah ride
Come to Jesus, baby. Come to Jesus

When those youngins get to Uni
So full of Jesus they cannot deny
if you tell them there's no one above
watching over them or hearing their prayers
They'll freak out and scream you lie
They'll tell their dipshit congressman
to get rid of the bad people who think about control
for themselves and know Jesus is a SCAM

Dragon Bodhing

Dragon has lived in Alabama, North Carolina, Missouri, Florida and Nevada before moving to Corpus Christi.

Excerpt from Baby Face

Testing and subject advancement were a growing concern among facility researchers, caretakers, and security. Anxiety lurked deep in the shadows. Many, if not most, were in the dark about the details pertaining to work at Miténas Scientific Research and Development Hall.

The Empaths believed that the withheld details intensified worry and caused a paranoid distraction for all participating and non-consenting employees. Yes, that argument could easily be made. However, the Others thrive in the evil lurking in the thick mischievous air, fueling unimaginable horrors. Not only fueling maliciousness but providing ideas with elaborate performances of destruction and rituals. Executing acts that would determine the state of humanity for decades to come and not for the best.

The unit had been built almost overnight. How it was constructed with such speed and mass in the brutal cold of this relatively new planet humans have infested, I cannot explain. From what I can recall, the concrete block loomed approximately 6 stories high with 3 towers, 1 on each corner. Two long rectangular buildings, a few flights shorter than the towers, connected the fourth corner. Though, it's hard to know for sure how many floors there really were from the lack of doors and windows. The long halls of the connecting rectangular buildings had windows on the top three levels; It should be noted that what I refer to as windows would hardly pass as such in the settings of suburban ticky-tacky homes or the corner office of whatever hamster wheel where the masses cling and abide. These attempted windows would serve a better purpose as mini ventilations. Perhaps that's what they were. The halls and floors were all identical. There was nothing regarding the floor one was on or the location in general. The purpose was to cause confusion. Every door was in the same spot, and tiles were cut and laid the exact same way for every floor with precision. Signs, room numbers, exits, doctors' office labels, and floor numbers were all absent. To get to a specific location promptly, or at all, one had to know, as a matter of fact, precisely where to go. If someone got lost, they simply weren't meant to be there and would be promptly exterminated. Each hall dangled three low-hanging pendant lights. The bulbs screwed in just enough to work yet maintain a constant nauseating flicker. And with each hall averaging a minimum of fifty feet long, one can understand how it would be easy to get lost and stay lost.

Dylan Lopez

Dylan Lopez is a graduate student at Texas A&M University-Corpus Christi. He is currently the Managing Editor of the *Windward Review* and President of the Islander Creative Writers.

Amusement Park

That's what they call it, when a motley caravan unfurls itself on the waterfront, revealing its revelry machines and costumed characters. Everyone comes down here in the summer months, a steady stream of sunny faces passing through the gates like an oceanside breeze. We parked far off in an empty lot, where two kids can share the last drags of a bittersweet year, laughing at graduation photos. She stayed behind a moment as I got out of the car and stared at the pictures like she was parsing through the ashes of our handiwork. In that pile, she found something that changed her cheery expression into something pained. I looked back at her, but knew not to ask--what changed.

She stayed with that sour look throughout our journey: on rusted roller coasters and aboard swinging ships, an air of disinterest followed, a tense shadow at my side. We played a dozen rounds of carny games and won handfuls of cheap stuffed prizes, but she maintained her sculpted look with stoic resolve--I wondered for a moment, if she left her smile in the car, in that pile of ashes.

As the day wore on my own joy cooled, I locked our fingers together, pulling us towards the park's last attraction with the vaguest of hopes. As the park's evening lights kicked on and the crowds began their exodus, we turned to the house of mirrors, which happily returned our view. The house of mirrors was my last chance, to know why this date went so poorly, why she couldn't enjoy our last day together.

I think I met her in there, for the first time. She was a fractal spirit, with a gaze that invited disaster. I couldn't see it clearly at first, but her sunflower locks parted as we stood there together, in every possible angle. I saw her a thousand times, in each one she looked at me through the mirrors, and in each one she wore the same face. Without parting her lips, she reminded me that this is what I wanted, even though I was warned; once for every paired reflection in that glass house. I never felt so small, as when she looked at me and said this was it. The park was closing, and this chapter of our lives was, too. In a few days she'd be on the road in that ragged car traveling to Oklahoma, but I was still stuck in high school. I wanted to reject that truth, and spend our last day together smiling, like the foolhardy outcast couple we were. She found that truth in those damn ashes, and was already thinking of "us" in the past tense.

I don't think I'll ever go to an amusement park again.

Monochromatic Monodies

The dull brush of heaven spread
Cross the sky, and drew all vibrancy
From the vista, save for a miserable slate

The tone of the great ash-fires was stricken,
And they burned a smoky tinge, ascending
Unto weeping clouds and starless infinities

Placid leviathans lost their course in the abyss,
And ran their colossal bodies aground; for alas,
Grey was the raging sea they called home

Soaring fowls turned from sublime heights,
As the hue of their ornate wings leapt forth,
And they fell longingly to the earth, disgraced

Elizabeth N. Flores

Elizabeth N. Flores, Professor Emeritus of Political Science, taught for 46 years at Del Mar College and was the college's first Mexican American Studies Program Coordinator. She was awarded the LULAC Council 1 Educator of the Year Award (2014) and the Del Mar College Dr. Aileen Creighton Award for Teaching Excellence (2013).

Treasure Chest

A cardboard box marked TREASURE CHEST,
filled with lollipops, rested on top of the
medicine cabinet in the examination room.

The doctor loved Corpus Christi's annual Buccaneer Days.
Framed posters of Buc Days' parades graced the wall
on both sides of the cabinet giving the Treasure Chest
even greater prominence.

You'd think at the age of ten I would have
outgrown the Treasure Chest.
But as the doctor examined me,
I kept my eyes on it.

"Just the old-fashioned flu," the doctor told Mama.
"She'll be fine in a few days."

The nurse, Lydia, smiled, brought the Treasure Chest down
from the cabinet and held it in front of me,
her beautiful charm bracelet lightly hitting against the box.
I scooped up three lollipops and something pointy.

It was a small crucifix.

I looked up at Mama, but her attention was on Lydia,
who was describing in detail her daughter's quinceanera.
"A blessing, but so much work, I'm glad it's over,"
Lydia said.

I put the lollipops and crucifix in my pocket.

I told Mama nothing about the crucifix.
I tucked it away in the shoebox where I kept my
First Holy Communion prayer book and holy card.

I didn't think about the crucifix very often,
but when I did I convinced myself
the doctor added prizes to the Treasure Chest.

A year later I had pink eye, so we went back to the doctor.
"You're such a good girl, pick five lollipops," Lydia said
as she presented me with the Treasure Chest.

She said lollipops! There were no prizes, only lollipops!
The crucifix did not belong to me!

What if it belonged to Lydia,
maybe a charm from her bracelet that she lost
when she was placing the candy in the Treasure Chest?

But what would happen if I showed the crucifix to Mama now,
a year after I brought it home?

I recovered from pink eye, but
my stomach ached and I could barely eat.

"We should go back to the doctor," Mama said.
"I'll call and make an appointment right now."

"No!" I yelled.

"Lydia will give you lollipops. You always love that,"
Mama said reassuringly, as she kissed the top of my head
and reached for the phone.

Ellissa Brewster

Ellissa Brewster was trained as a journalist at Texas A&M University. Most of her writing career was related to public relations. She also worked as writing tutor at Del Mar College. During her retirement years, she is having fun experimenting with family stories, personal memoir, and poetry.

Letting Go

An indiscernible snap
Detached,
I am Free!

Dry and crisp
Busy greenness gone.

Silently, carelessly
Twirling my multi-colored dress
around
Around
around.

Released from
then and what if.
Down,
Down
down

Autumn breezes and gravity
choreograph my
s
w
i
r
l
i
n

g

into Now.

Grace finds
loving hands to carry me.
Wet but afloat
I surrender to current.

Drifting white puffs on blue above
Furtive water creatures below
Ephemeral bubbles sail and pop

Shadow patterns shift
as cousins
release and fall
to join my water dance.
Steady
Stones
Give
(With persistent kindness, Pause
the current pries me loose.)

A melody of Earth essences,
Cool shade pockets
Delicate sunray rainbows
Quiet joy
At rest now.
My destined spot
on the bank
thick with damp.
Peace
I return to You, Mother
To enrich earth
to fade to new life.
No longer one.
Many and Whole,
I am Yours.
Surrender

Esther Bonilla Read

Esther Bonilla Read is a retired teacher. Now she is a fulltime writer. In 2022 TCU Press published her book, *After the Blessing*, in which Mexican-American veterans of WWII tell their own stories. One of her stories, The Ring, is featured in the book, *Chicken Soup for the Latino Soul*. She has also been published in newspapers and various anthologies.

What it Means to Retire

I had been retired five years when my husband decided to retire. I was relieved. We could travel, eat dinner on time, and just take it easy. Then, the school system called me to be a substitute.

"I'll have dinner waiting for you when you get home," my husband said to me as I left on the first day. After all, our roles were now reversed.

That was all right with me. While I enjoy cooking, a vacation might be nice…I thought to myself as I drove to my job. When I arrived home that first day and saw a nice meatloaf waiting to be eaten, I smiled…not bad for someone who doesn't know how to cook. "What is the white stuff in the middle?" I asked.

"Oh, that's oatmeal. The recipe said half a cup, and I decided to use two cups."

In an effort to not dampen his spirits I said, "Now you've cooked a little bit in your life, but there is something you need to know. You are not at the level in cooking that allows you to improvise. Some ingredients, if misused, do odd things to food. So next time don't deviate from the recipe."

"We can freeze the leftovers and eat them later," he said enthusiastically. I nodded and when he wasn't looking, I threw away the whole disgusting thing.

The following day, when I arrived from my substituting job, he beamed, "We have pizza tonight, six of them"

"Why six?"

"Because that is what the recipe called for. Remember…you said, 'Don't deviate from the recipe'".

"Right," I answered and called neighbors to see who hadn't had dinner. The next day I delighted the staff with two pizzas for lunch.

On the following day I arrived home to find he had made soup in a twelve-quart container. I tried to distinguish one vegetable from another. "What did you put in the soup?" I asked.

"Well, besides the meat, about five vegetables, and then, I cooked it for hours!"

Another short lesson about the different required cooking time of meat and vegetables, and I didn't even approach the idea of halving a recipe. Why address so many issues at once?

Upon ironing my pants, I found my khaki pants had black spots on them and my black pants had white spots on them. "Don't ever wash my clothes," I pleaded. "I'll do the washing when I get home."

On another occasion I arrived home to find the kitchen door propped open with a chair. "What happened? Flies will come in."

"I burned dinner," my husband admitted. "Do you mind?"

"Not at all," I answered. "It'll be nice to go out to eat."

Finally, my substitute job ended. My husband asked, "Do you still want me to cook from time to time just to give you a break?"

"No," I answered. "It's good to be back at this job." I looked in the refrigerator and found packages and bowls of stored food utilizing every inch of space available. The pantry, also, displayed shelf after shelf of canned food all the way to the back- GALLON containers of mustard, mayonnaise, and tomatoes, cans of this and that and who knows what sat at the back of the shelves. I didn't even want to find out.

"If the substitute office calls looking for me", I yelled from the pantry, "tell them I left town."

"Why, is anything wrong?' he responded.

"No," I answered.

I could have wept!

F.E.I.

F.E.I. prefers to write in an open room as if the stories emerge from the physical space. After moving to Corpus Christi, she found that it has more space than she had hoped.

Super Singularity

At his retirement party, I was told by the affable man that I cried all the way from Chicago to Corpus, and my mother had asked if he would like to hold the bottle for me so she could use the bathroom. He had rosy apple cheeks that make you believe Norman Rockwell was a realist. He was my mother's boss, but I'd never formally met him until then. What a dizzy scene.

On perhaps the same exact short rattling plane, I was aware that I cried again. This would be my summer without Ian. He announced his engagement on an auditing trip, getting down on one knee with a Tiffany solitaire, on top of an Indian burial rock that apparently took them four hours to reach. Of course, I unfriended both.

My mother never really worked after that fateful plane ride, if you call bringing up me as working, then she kept both of us busy. Supposedly every passenger who walked past took a good look at me. "God made babies cute for very practical reasons." The old man was a joker, but I had no doubt. Mother is doing fine without me. When she did call, I was suspicious. When we ran out of weather reports, she said she might appreciate some help. Her English is a bit distant and always formal. She didn't have anyone to speak Chinese with since I chose to learn Spanish just to spite her. I retained a handful of childhood words but worried I would sound juvenile.

"What did you do, mommy?"

"What did I do? Nothing! Just getting out of bed, and heard the knee went click. Well, glad that part was over. Well, I called around and found a rental at Bayview. You haven't seen my place, but I have no room."

She has room. I am just messy. If we are in each other's exclusion zones of operation, we adjust like two metal beads toying with the antithesis of polar charges. Only when she sees her physical therapist, I am the center piece of the Venn diagram.

This is a new city that we visited here once jointly, me, being two months old, really didn't care. Being an expert rationalist, she somehow surprised me by settling here. "I can live anywhere." She gave me free reign of the shadeless living room. "I am getting hummingbirds around here all the time. Can you believe it? They are marvelous! We should go to Gill's to pick up some plants."

When I saw her therapist called her inside, I settled back into the seat off of the front door. A lady across the floor from me next to the water cooler scanned me with her cool blue eyes. Her turmeric turban wrapped high, cutting her petite frame a grand figure. Her floral cane neatly sat by her chair.

"Heard this place is hard to book…Are you feeling better?" I said, since our eyes met already.

"Me? Oh no! I'm a worried mother tagging along with my son. He is inside." She gestured with her sparkling eyes. They looked proud when she said "my son." She opened a soft skinned purse by her hip and pulled out a neatly folded mask as she was about to cough. She wired the elastic around her face and said apologetically:

"Excuse me. Shoulda covered up the moment I came in. This is from my grandson. Just got into the air force. Send me a bunch of these. Said grandma should wear the top gun stuff!" She chuckled.

A dark, long-limbed man came out and grinned. The lady reached out to his hand, looked like she'd been leaning onto him to raise herself out of a chair for the one hundredth time, but quickly she realized her son was on a crutch, so she attempted to struggle alone. The son shook his head and gave me a knowing smile.

"See, she doesn't trust me!"

"You are right my son. That's why mama must come all the way here to see if you are doing a good job!"

"Ms. Michelle said I did a good job, ma. I am taking good care of myself. And I am thirty-eight!" He winked at me with such glee.

She relented and held on to his hand tightly.

My mother came out right at the point I was about to doze off, at two-thirty.

"Take me to Little Chinatown on Holly." She must have spent a fortune there. She bought ten types of tofu, lotus roots, bottles and cans of pastes and deadly bundles of tiny red peppers. The little strip mall is like a windsock that catches everything: candy wrappers, soda bottles, lidded Styrofoam cups with straws stuck in them, swirling on the ground trying to make a mark in this corner of the world. Ian would have liked here better than the gentrified Chinatown in D.C.

I started a braised tofu pot with black mushrooms, plugged in the rice cooker I just bought. According to mother's instructions, I also washed some millet and wrinkly dates for a porridge. I was rushing and didn't want to miss the happy hour.

The flight school cadets had towels, beach balls and plates of grilled chicken thighs balanced on their glistening arms below my window. There were children with floaties hugged their limbs, and their tanned moms strolling in with canvas totes, ready to set up camp. So much sun burnt athleticism on display. The latissimus and rhomboids came up and down like whales diving for air. Their laughs punctuated the quietness and eventually dissipated along with the color blocking towels that wrapped around anonymous bouncy shoulders, walking slowly against the blinding setting sun, leaving behind the lone agave beyond the locked gate.

I woke up with a start, unfurling my legs from the stiff surfaced sofa. The low humming from the naval planes was relentless in their night flights. The orange light on the rice cooker looks like a lighting bug looking for the perfect patch of night. The pot will be all warm and syrupy in my car on its way to mother's when the morning begins.

Gerald Beckman

Gerald Beckman is a retired attorney. Three of his novels are on Amazon. This book will be available in early 2024.

St. Anskar's Murder

Pick the right road leading southwest out of San Antonio and stick with it long enough, and you'll eventually arrive in Falcon. You'll know it's Falcon when you see the spire of St. Anskar's in the distance, soaring above the one- and two-story buildings surrounding it in the middle of the town, like a mother hovering over a brood of well-behaved children.

The town is as different from San Antonio as it's possible to get. Small, uninteresting, caught in the backwaters of time; nothing of interest had happened there since its founding in the late 1800's. About 2000 people call it home, a number that hasn't changed much in the last 100 years. It was a great place to retire if you like peace and quiet, and peace and quiet is what I was looking for when I quit chasing drug smugglers for the DEA in Corpus Christi. Thirty-five years matching wits with big time hoodlums and their minions is long enough for anybody, and for me it was too long.

The church was built in1909, much too grand for a small cowtown like Falcon. But it's there, and most people thought it would be there forever. Tall and majestic, it's visible for miles from all directions. Solid granite, with stained glass windows all around, it causes people passing through to wonder why, way the hell-and-gone out here in the middle of nowhere, was a thing like this built? For what? For whom? Sometimes curiosity is strong enough for a stranger to stop for a closer look, to walk around the church, stare at the bell tower where hangs a real bell that somebody actually rings on occasion; and if the church is open, step inside and gaze at the impressive, bright colored windows and murals, not to mention marble statues and paintings.

Its history is no secret. There's a stack of slick-paper folders on a stand inside the front door, full of details and free for the taking, telling when it was built, how long it took, where the granite came from and how it arrived in wagon trains straight from the quarry, the name of the benefactor whose money paid for the whole thing, the names of all priests assigned there since the beginning, the name of the Bishop under whose direction it was built, where in Italy the paintings and marble statues came from; all but the reason for the grandeur is proudly told right there in black and white and full-color photographs.

The reason for the grandeur is no secret either, though it's nowhere written or recorded. It's just not a subject that holds folks' interest much any more. Until the oil boom started bringing in service trucks by the dozens to tear up the streets, and hard-hatted roughnecks with tattooed biceps flashing enough money to disrupt the economy, most of the locals had enough problems wresting a living from the semi-arid brushland without wasting a lot of effort on a piece of history whose revival might rile certain folks better left un-riled.

And so the church is still just there, unchanging and unchangeable, a major but part of the psyche of everybody. Nobody questions it, nobody wonders too much about it. It's just there, the site of countless weddings, funerals, socials, mass everyday and twice on Sundays. But in recent years its importance has been waning. It's been limping along on a slim budget getting slimmer every year, but nothing exciting happens. Ever.

Until some unknown perp saw fit to bash Nichol Sommer's brains out while she was sitting in her car in the church parking lot. That brought more excitement than most folks wanted to deal with. It happened during a banquet the parishioners were giving at the parish hall to celebrate Monsignor John Ray's 25th anniversary to the priesthood. John was one of my classmates at St. Anskar's High School in the old days.

Jacob R. Benavides

Jacob R. Benavides holds a BA in English from TAMU-CC and is pursuing an MFA in Creative Writing. He seeks to contribute to the conversations of form and feeling in a Queer South Texas existence.

Imitation/Immature

Wet.
ribbon curls 'round all,
unfurling lovely shiver stars...

Fitting candle wick to bruise
Bushes in bloom, little monsoons
this time, I'll give my hyacinth's room To feel To grip
the Earth--
then upend,
Upside down and Greedy bent for every bit
Of him. Tethered to be tender once more
Let this love be a sinew.

Climbing up the candle stick, popping wicks
unwound like twisting stones, stripped peach pits
sinking deeper into the shelter of him,
Soft cramp earthquake of my veins
Cradle Me.
Let this love be a sinew.

Every burgeoning sun is an ashcake,
Coal baked into the stoic air of a window,
Bending outwards pulled in
Fractured tones draped in muscle, paraffin
vessel, vibrant bones, youthful hue
practicing softness once again
Let this love be a sinew,
and from this sinew, I'll untie a muscle,
Undo.

[*Beat.*]

Jacqueline Gonzalez

Jacqueline Gonzalez is a Corpus Christi native and developed a love of writing at a very young age. She holds a BA in English from TAMUCC and a MA in English and Creative Writing from SNHU. Jacqueline works as a Staff Writer at Visit Corpus Christi and is also a Contributing Writer for The Bend Magazine. Read more of her work at MaysPublishing.com or at **www.jacquelinejisele.com**

A Young Woman Left for Dead

Eyes lined with purple and black,
Her lips a striking blood red.
A tear-stained face and a broken heart,
A young woman left for dead.

She lay still on the floor,
As the color drained from her face.
He tried to hold her close,
But he was met with a cold embrace.

Her eyes wouldn't open,
No movement in her body.
He tried holding her hand,
And received cold stares from everybody.

He didn't mean to swing so hard,
But he couldn't take it back.
He stared at her lifeless body,
As his entire existence faded to black.

J. L. Wright

J. L. Wright, a recent boomerang resident of Corpus Christi, is an internationally published poet. Most recently published by the International Women's Writers Guild in 2022, J. L. Is currently working on their third poetry collection. J. L. is committed to live the life of a poet, observing and documenting the voice of the people.

Epoxy

Elmers eaten by roaches
Silverfish do the rest
photos released from pages
on which they were pressed
albums forgotten
faces drop to box bottoms
packed memories unglued

ambered black and white glossies
stained and curled corners
families pecking your brain
someone loved unknown
thrown in a fire
or shellacked upon a shelf
as a tribute to desire

JoAnn Sanderson

JoAnn Sanderson received a Master's Degree in English Education at Southern University and taught in Illinois public schools for many years. After retiring, she lived in Corpus Christi for over twenty years.

When Opportunity Knocks

If I told you my story "slant," as Emily Dickinson suggests, I doubt you would be sympathetic to my situation. But if you read my story with a discerning mind, I trust you to regard me kindly because I have been honest and have indicated my intent to mend my ways, although you may think I don't show sufficient remorse. You might adopt a "wait and see" stance. But, if you do, at least, you would be giving me another chance.

When my husband, Rodney, told me we had been invited to dinner at the home of the head of Binkman Auditors, LLP, his employer, I was delighted. "Another opportunity," I thought. "But, Rodney, of course, I'll have to shop for something appropriate to wear. Something fashionable but dignified. Something that would impress both Leonora Binkman and her husband."

"Something fashionable, dignified, and within our budget," Rodney replied as he pulled out his wallet and handed me four fifty dollar bills. "And remember to give me the receipt for our records."

Before Rodney and I were married six months ago, my parents warned me that my profligate spending would cause problems. They reminded me often of my, as they put it, former "missteps" while walking on the wild side during my high school and college years. Mom and Dad looked at each other, worried glances emanating from their eyes as Rodney and I told them our plans.

I assured them I knew Rodney is frugal and persnickety, but now I am a person who knows that problems are invitations to seek opportunities to seek solutions. "Don't worry so much. I have a lucrative position as a graphic designer at Go Graphics, Incorporated. I'm a responsible adult now."

Rodney, however, took the first step to avoid rather than solve potential problems. After Rodney insisted, I agreed to close my individual credit card account. However, I intended to find creative ways to modify this restriction. My problem-solving skills are clever and bold rather than methodical and punitive, as are my well-meaning husband's.

Rodney is the firm's newest hire. He is intelligent, persuasive, but not sufficiently paid for his service—yet. I am determined to help Rodney climb the ladder of financial success. And now this dinner gives me an opportunity to help him take a step forward to becoming a partner in Binkman Auditors, LLP. I am determined, in my soon-to-be beautiful new dress, to charm the Brinkmans.

"Thanks, Dear. I'm sure I'll be able to find something you will like," I looked at the four fifty dollar bills he handed me," for 200 dollars."

You see, Rodney could interpret tax codes and verify financial statements, but did not understand the nuances of networking and the social milieu of auditors. These were my specialties.

Before I set off to select a dress at the moderately priced Xavier's Designer Salon, Rodney reminded me, "You know I want you to look great, but you must stay within the budget. Besides, you look great in anything."

I interpreted his words as a warning ameliorated by a compliment.

The day after he told me about the dinner invitation, I walked into Xavier's Salon wearing tan, straight leg Ponte knit joggers, a white waffle-knit sweater, carrying my cappuccino-colored leather tote bag.

The three sales clerks were helping other customers, so I had time to peruse the offerings, select five items, and take them into the dressing room, although I was interested in only two of them.

I tried on the $180 Susan Elders dusty blue knit fit and flair dress. I decided it was spunky, but wouldn't be too threatening to dowdy Leonora Brinkman. Then I tried on the Cassie Lee $420 chiffon dress printed with vertical swirls of cream and grey stripes. This dress looked great on me—sophisticated, yet sexy. Looking directly at my reflection in the dressing room mirror, I defied an imagined Leonora, "Too bad, Leonora, you'll just have to deal with it."

Then I remembered the $200 in my wallet and Rodney's directive. There I was in a dressing room at Xavier's Designer Salon being tested in a trial by fire—a problem inviting an opportunity to solve my dilemma.

I removed the chiffon dress, took the fit and flair to the sales clerk, handed her four fifty dollar bills, put the $5.60 change in my wallet (I knew he'd count the change), and left the store.

At five o'clock I arrived home, went directly to the bedroom, shut the door, removed the carefully folded $180 dusty blue fit and flair from its box and laid it on the bed. Then I emptied the item in my tote bag—the $420 cream and grey striped Cassie Lee chiffon. As I held it up against my body to admire it in my full length mirror, I announced, "When opportunity knocks, you must open the door. I am a very savvy partner of a man who will soon be a partner in Binkman Corporation, LLP."

But then I looked at the dusty blue fit and flair laying on the bed. I picked it up, held it against my body, and looked again at my reflection in the mirror. "Wow, this dress is great, too! Maybe I didn't need to jeopardize my future and Rodney's by engaging in this escapade, after all. Rodney and I agree: I look great in anything—anything but an orange jump suit." I laid the dusty blue fit and flair beside the cream and grey striped chiffon on the bed.
As I stood beside the bed looking down at my newly-acquired possessions, I heard footsteps outside the bedroom, followed by three soft taps on the door. Rodney opened the door and announced, "I got off early today, Honey. Looks like you've been shopping."
He walked toward the two dresses lying side by side, each with an attached price tag attracting the scrutiny of an auditor's eye. I saw the disappointment in his eyes when he asked me for the receipt. I know he knew what I had done. I handed it to him, and he took it to his office.

And there you have it, reader. This story hasn't ended yet. Rodney is in his office recording my personal assets and liabilities, my strengths and my weaknesses, what I have deposited and what I have withdrawn from the Bank of Marital Expectations. He's doing a risk management assessment. Being savvy and clever, I won't interrupt him.

As for me, I don't have to record anything in a ledger. He identified the problem, as auditors do. But I had already figured out how to solve it just by looking in the mirror.

Nicole Serrao

Mi Amore

Joel Ortiz

Joel Jay Ortiz has been reading, writing, and performing poetry since 1991. He started at various open mikes, reading poetry with musicians, and then continued when open mike with spoken word began appearing. The following are excerpts from ***Corpitos: A Sadness***

Dos Veces Mojado

Jose was riding his bicycle already drunk
On two six packs & one on his handlebars
This time he's been here six months
Saving money, clothes, electronics, & drunken
Endeavors to mask his loneliness in this
Cold country; in a bad part of town
Their lights on, the *jura,* as he calls them,
Chase him down, & he from another country,
From another time & from different expectations
Gets scared and runs.
The *jura* in this city likes to jump first as if
They are modern Texas Rangers doing their job
& they catch up with Jose & first they tase him
Surprising him to fall on the floor & then they
Jump him & beat him for evading arrest
Jose doesn't understand their speech as they
Bark orders at his bloody face. He's taken to
The hospital to be stitched up, then he's taken
To the detention center to be locked up.
Two weeks later, his body still aches with
Bruises, he still doesn't know why he's
Incarcerated & his only thoughts are of his
Wife & daughter who he hasn't spoken to
Since this ordeal began & he wonders if they
Wonder if he's dead as they are safe at
Home in Guatemala.

The Dirtiest animal de Robe

Can you help me write something please, can you help me write a letter
To the judge *por favor*
I want to tell my side of the story homie, I want my side to be said, and
I think the judge should hear it from me

These are all memories of my dead friends
And the power we have with our dead friends
So the 22 of February, is right around the corner
What breaths am I feeling right now, what
Masks are being lifted for me, the veil
Is loose right now, what is it you
Are trying to tell me

I've got this, let me write it out
Let me write out my dreams
From the stabbing to the kid
Running around the office,
It all comes from somewhere
Even the faces we see in the night air,
Spirits wanting an ear, begone from me

Driving a car, picking a rose,
Breaking the antennae, finding a point
Underneath the street I beat my feet
Digging ahole, crashing into corn
Buying a magazine filled with porn
Finding that love, orgasmagical climes,
Reading Baudelaire at that opportune time
Asking one question, for once in your life
Hitting a b flat on wine glass chimes
Becoming a man is easy while regressing becomes sublime
In front of everyone we all must cry
It's inevitable because we all must die.

Joseph Wilson

Joseph Wilson taught Advanced Placement Senior English, Film Studies, and Creative Writing at Richard King High School for 42 years. He has been a driving force in the advancement of the arts and literacy in the Coastal Bend.

Hanging Prayer

I almost can't believe that it has been
Over two years since my beautiful mother died
Down in Fort Myers during the pandemic
Not from Covid but from pitched battles with ~~old age~~ cancer
~~Cancer~~ And old age ~~and~~ until various systems shut ~~hutting~~ down
I didn't fly to Florida ~~because of~~

~~My fears~~ I was afraid about traveling from Texas and contracting
The disease but I got it later twice and survived
My brother and two sisters gave witness
And comfort huddling around my mother's ~~her~~ deathbed
Holding her hands and soothing her forehead
My sister Beth lifted ~~held~~ the iPhone above her so I could

Tell mom "I love you" but she was cinched up
Semi-conscious and said "Joe" like a moan or question
With her voice going up on the "e" at the end of my name
When she died the next day
I was of course sad and ashamed and relieved
That I didn't share the messy burden of her last moments

At dusk in my front yard I strung high a set of Tibetan prayer
Flags between two branches of a downed mesquite
Tree that had split off   fallen because of high wind
Now last night two years later the line broke
Not for the first time the once brightly colored flags were
Earthbound, frayed, dulled, and the various Buddhist

Mantras erased by storms and time and breezes
I am not a Buddhist
I don't believe much of anything spiritual
Or mythological beyond the genuine linkages
That we humans ~~beings~~ invest thought and feelings in
But every instance ~~hour~~ when the fabric flags ~~s~~ spin and flap ~~in~~
~~the strong and steady (adjectives that fit my mother) [Joe, consider if this fits her] South Texas breeze [tells the reader where you are; it was a long trip to see your Mom; you were not anywhere nearby]~~

I think of my kind mother Mary Marie and her animated
Good life   so today I hang a new collection of ~~twenty~~ 20 fourteen
By fourteen inch blue, white, red, green, yellow linen squares
With Sanskrit words embossed in silver and gold
Koans__ which I cannot decode   decorated with images of tiger, lion
Horse, dragon   all metaphors for blessings that fly
~~metaphors that in context are mysteries~~

Sunday, March 5, 2023 then March 7 then March 26 Draft 17 ~~Draft 13~~//font is American Typewriter Comments by Tim Dowling

Listening to David Crosby

Back on Ewing Street
When I was a teenage boy home from college
I spun records by Crosby Stills Nash and Young
On my Yamaha turntable
In my bedroom
At the top of the stairs
I played the music so loud
That my mother purchased ear plugs
And eventually
Bought me corded headphones

Tethered to my space
I spread myself out
Flat on my back
On the hooked green rug
Like I was a huge Coca-Cola spill
Cover art and liner notes
Pressed to my chest like love letters
My eyes closed to the ceiling light
And my mind open to the inner
Correspondences of song

This morning on the drive into school
I listen to David Crosby on Sirius Radio
Being interviewed by Terry Gross
About his life as a working musician
About his romantic relationship with Joni
About his heroin addiction and liver transplant
About his collaboration with his son on his new cd
About his upcoming 73rd birthday in August

Cros ends the "Fresh Air" chat with this
Most declarative of sentences:
"Music is love"
I nod my head yes
Several times yes
As if I were an acolyte
Sitting in a scented garden
Singing harmony

William Mays

Deserted Street at Midnight

Judy Bloomquist

Judy Bloomquist is a Kinesiology lecturer at Texas A&M-Kingsville. Her book, *The Misfits Become a Pack,* is based on her love of rescue animals.

Excerpt from *The Misfits Become a Pack*

I am Molly the Weiner dog, I was the first member of the current pack and am also the oldest. I have long hair with a really long body that almost scrapes the ground. I am kind of funny looking but I am a fierce leader. I want to tell you the story of how I became the leader of a very special pack. I used to live on a farm where puppies were made. There were always dogs everywhere running and barking and playing. It was a great place to live. One day a lady came to our farm looking for something. The farmer suggested that she sit down in a chair in the yard and just look around a while at all the puppies. It was a fun place and she seemed to enjoy all my puppy friends being puppies. I decided to get a closer look at the lady so I snuck under her chair. I think I scared the lady because she suddenly looked down at me with big eyes and a huge smile. I think she liked me. She said I was the cutest little Weiner dog she had ever seen. She was just sitting there looking at me as if to say, "Do you want to come home with me? I told the lady, I'm your girl". I think the lady must speak "bark" because she called the farmer over and said, "I'll take this one!". She put me in a car and drove me to her house and that was the start of my new pack.

She gave me the name Molly but the humans often called me "Mol Mol". When I arrived at my new house, I didn't know what to expect. A fluffy old chihuahua approached me with a look of attack, but the dog was so old and weak she forgot what she was growling at and went to lay down. My humans called her "Quince" and spoiled her and loved her very much. A couple days later I went out to the back yard and found my humans digging a big hole in the dirt. When they were done digging, they put a bundle wrapped in a blanket in the hole and began to weep. I heard one human say "goodbye".

I was confused until I went in the house looking for Quince and she was nowhere to be found. I realized that it was her in the hole that the humans were crying over. I also realized that it was my turn to lead this pack and protect my new humans. I wanted to prove my loyalty. I was very protective of my new house and family. I barked at all unfamiliar noises to show them that I was in charge and protecting them. Just to prove my fearlessness, one day I nipped at our neighbor's heels because she came into our house without warning. I had to prove to them this was my house now. My human in charge (I call The Lady) scolded me and apologized to our neighbor.

But I think she was secretly proud of me for taking a stand. At least I think that's what the treat was for that she snuck to me under the table…

Jill Scott

Husband in the Haystack

Judy Mastenbrook

Judy Mastenbrook worked as a teacher and counselor for children from early childhood through seventh grade. She went on to teach at the college level. She passed away with complications from Parkinson's disease in January 2023.

After I Die

After I die, my dresser drawers will be filled with well-worn sexy underwear, including the camisole with imported lace.

After I die, the soles of all my shoes will be scuffed, even the red sequined shoes on the top shelf, inappropriate for almost every occasion.

After I die, appalled collectors will quietly condemn my practice of covering my beds with my antique quilts, none will be folded in tissue paper in dark closets.

After I die, the set of dishes inherited from my mother, never seen before her death, will be found on the dining room table with the remains of my last meal.

After I die, books on spirit matters, mysteries, antiques, weaving, and poetry will be found on my bookshelves, while books on efficiency and the stock market will weigh down someone else's shelf.

After I die, no boxes of scented soaps will be left waiting to be used.

After I die, the shabby furniture will not be worth inheriting, but the art on the walls will be a feast for other lucky eyes.

After I die, it will be apparent, my living was used up...

William Mays

Vulture (Buzzard)

Karen Cline-Tardiff

Karen has been writing as long as she could hold a pen. She is founder and Editor-in-Chief of Gnashing Teeth Publishing. Find her at **karenthepoet.com**

Buzzard

You look at me
  think I'm ugly

Do you not see the
  beauty   my vermillion head
  black and grey feathers iridescent

Talons curved   curled
   cradled around the line

Graceful   balanced
   I hold my wings aloft
   dry them in the wind

You see scavenger   hunter
   eater of dead flesh

I am necessary
   designed by nature
      beautiful to behold

Until you tell me I am not

Sister Lou Ella Hickman

Sister Lou Ella Hickman's works have appeared in numerous magazines and anthologies. She was nominated for the Pushcart Prize in 2017 and in 2020.

the legend of the turquoise stone

one day
when father sky wept
his tears fell into mother earth
he wept for so many days
the tears became a river
our mother the earth let the river run
and the river became many rivers
watering our land
the river slept
while the sun and the moon
danced and sang
traveling
their journey for many years
while the tears slowly
rivered into stone
one day
the stone whispered
to our ancestors
let me be beauty for you
wrap me with a ribbon of silver
wear me
for i am a gift from father sky
a gift from mother earth born

elizabeth bishop and georgia o'keeffe

they could have been sisters
how alike but different
one whose palette was singularly
sensuous as her desert
the other with her art of losing
painted poems
and stories shimmering with color

o'keeffe speaks:

ignore that my husband said
my flowers were a woman's body part
as well as what my commentators
and critics wrote
my secret is something more
so much more

bishop speaks:

my wandering
was restless as the sea
in my brittle thirst
for what i could never find
i gave my body away . . .
loss became my art and words
until my final loss found me
whose name is home . . .
oh, yes
my secret is more

so

much

more

Jeff Janko

Rocking Chair in Front of a Window

John Meza

Self-portrait
At Work

John Meza

John Meza writes poetry—and builds bridges.

Was not time wasted

If only your rejection
Tasted as sweet
As your belly at 2 am
Maybe this Maker's neat
Would not be drowning
My sorrows

If only I could read to you
All the poems I've written
To your absence
Knowing
You didn't love me
Maybe you would understand
My devotion

If only, everything
That happened in the last
113 days
Since you called me for help
Meant more to you
Than it did to me
Maybe I could forget counting
97 hairs on the upper eyelash
Of your left eye
As you slept

If only, you had told me
Eight years ago
You didn't know
How to love
Maybe I could have spent
The time trying to find
Someone who could
Rather than spend the last
3302 days pining away for you
Only to have you say no
For a second time

If only, being loved
Was not time wasted

Juan Manuel Pérez

Juan Manuel Perez, a Mexican-American poet of indigenous descent, was the Poet Laureate of Corpus Christi from 2019-2021. He has written several books of poetry. He worships his Creator and chases chupacabra in South Texas.

Sounds Of Easter Weekend
La Rosita by Stony Brook Park, Corpus Christi, Texas
Friday-Sunday, April 2-4, 2021

Good Friday indeed
we planted a rose garden
wife's new pride and joy

shovel's communion
slicing through virgin-fresh dirt
bejeweling roses

hummingbirds fighting
long-dead-tree territory
feeders for earrings

wild birds carry on
feeding time long overdue
wife pulls out bird seed

the sounds of Easter
people playing volleyball
noisy, nearby park

cascarones' war
two sides lined up for battle
everybody wins

kids throwing softballs
a busy, green Sunday park
watching from my lawn

Half The World On A Monday: Living With Limited Sight
Alice High School, Alice, Texas
Monday, April 5, 2021

a life through one eye
camera two malfunctioning
running into walls

half of the "hellos"
only seen through the right eye
get half a "goodbye"

waiting for a turn
to turn and turn all around
without falling down

way past this long mess
all surgeries placed on hold
frustration building

one eye understands
normal sight is luxury
depression looming

if I could only…
read a book like I used to
fleeting happiness

I know I missed it
half of the world on Monday
second half Tuesday

The Incident
La Rosita, Corpus Christi, Texas
Friday, March 11, 2022

a normal morning
showered, shaved, going to work
a prayer for breakfast

opening my eyes
black snakes evolving within
getting hard to see

the doctor's office:
something went terribly wrong
life changing event

told me to relax
a microaneurysm
right eye injection

now both eyes don't work
what am I going to do
on medical leave

how did this happen
high stress or diabetes?
self-imposed prison

if I only knew
that I would end up this way
it can't end like this

John Pettigrove

A retired physician, John Pettigrove spends his time writing—and fishing. Look for his book *Run of the Tide* on Amazon.

Excerpt from *Run of the Tide*

Bill Fant, a Corpus Christi radiologist, had a passion for the outdoors. Like the Karankawa Indians, he loved fishing for redfish and Spotted Sea Trout, especially in the Laguna Madre. For Bill, fishing meant sight fishing. His fishing methods were simple. He used sparse tackle and carried only a handful of lures in his shirt pocket. His method was to hunt the fish on their own turf. He could stalk for hours, walking the sea grass meadows, sand bars and mud flats. If you were a young angler and wanted to learn his methods, he welcomed you to come along and learn.

The first time I fished with Bill was in 1974. His fishing partner in those days was Jim Moser, a tough burley man who worked for the Southern Pacific Railroad. On my first trip with them, it was a hot July summer morning. Roy Grassedonio and Dr. Bert Garcia accompanied us. We launched at Jerry's Place off Laguna Shores in Flour Bluff and traveled at top speed down the intracoastal in Bill's seventeen foot Mako sport fishing boat. On the way down the lagoon we passed Jim's son, Chester, who had gotten off to an earlier start. Chester was standing in calf deep water along the intercostal at old marker seventy-five, a place now called the miracle bar. He was holding up an almost yard long Speckled Trout as we sped past. I could tell right then I was going to like Bill's' kind of fishing.

We banked the boat and walked slowly along the shore. Bill had me keep close so he could "introduce me to the fish." He would glide silently thorough the water looking this way, and then that, checking every speck of grass and dark spot on the sand for a sign of a fin, a shadow, a wake or a tail. I followed bumbling and sloshing along. Bill would occasionally kindly admonish me for making too much noise, point out a fish here and there, and encourage me to cast. At first I did not get it and was usually looking in the wrong place. He would make a cast, just like a forward pass right into the mouth of a waiting fish I never saw until it was on the line.

As the day went by I began to sense the reality of it. He wasn't making this up and there really were fish out there, albeit at first, invisible to me. And then it happened I began seeing fish in the water. Bill would say if you think you see something, anything don't take your eyes off it until you think you are going blind. I began to realize that sometimes he saw a whole fish in the clear water but mostly he saw a fin, some shine of a side, an out of place movement or a shadow on the bottom. Sometimes I was fooled and some of those first redfish and trout were in reality big horse Mullet or Hard Head Catfish. But I learned and gained confidence and became hooked for a lifetime.

When I asked him how he got started fishing in Texas, he said when he first came to the Texas Gulf Coast he just watched people. He hung out at Jerry's Place in Flour Bluff standing around, talking to anglers about who the best fishermen were and watched until one of those men left in his boat. Often, he would hop in his skiff and take off following at a distance until he found where they went and how they fished. He never got close enough so they were ever on to him. There was this one man Andy Anderson. When Bill met him, Andy was an old man. He was the master in those days but so secretive that no one knew what his game was. He would come in from fishing with a boat full of trout and red fish, sometimes selling them at the Fish House. Bill tried everything to get to know old Anderson but with no success. Anderson was tough and naturally secretive. He would have none of Bill's dockside conversation.

When the old man left the boat ramp at dawn Bill had been at the dock for at least an hour and had putted his skiff out in the dark waiting on him. Then, Bill would follow Anderson at a distance and watch him closely through binoculars until he learned the best spots in the upper lagoon and enough technique that he could begin to develop his own strategies. After a time, Anderson quit fishing and Bill never saw him again. He never knew why Anderson quit coming and no one at the marina could tell him. Bill told me he just guessed some anglers were like that in the old days, had mysterious ways and died with their secrets. And that's how Bill got started learning from a man he never really knew.

It wasn't long after Anderson was gone that people started following Bill and for good reason because after Bill and Jim Moser began fishing together they soon became known as two of the best and had become experts in their own right.

John Morris/Michelle Zudrell

John Morris takes stunning large-scale photographs of seascapes and writes poetic commentary about what he sees. Michelle Zudrell is a painter/photographer/jewelry maker and the Gallery Director at the Port Aransas Art Center. Together, they started working on *Bookmarks*, which combines photography, poetry, and commentary.

An excerpt from *Bookmarks*

We're writing about us, but it's more than that…we write of a journey, not a destination, but instead of a path we chose…happiness. As we travel the path, we find that it's a path full of discoveries, the score of little things that we share, that we do, that we experience together that makes us…"us." A shared love of art and the outdoors, a natural ability to feel connected on so many levels…to know deep down inside what we each feel, and what we need, and to somehow share this journey in a way that may help us and help others…to simply find happiness.

We finish each other's unspoken thoughts. When Michelle gave me a journal, we decided we'd share it…a place to capture our thoughts, our ideas, our dreams. Ultimately a kernel of an idea grew…could we write a book, our story, a cautionary tale, and maybe an inspiration…to simply chose happiness.

Bookmark - Start the Journey

Where do we start? Is it really on page one…or is it that we really begin…or begin anew as we finish a chapter. Just one waypoint on our journey, and we turn the page. A fresh start…shaped by all the previous chapters…waypoints.
11.6.2022

Where does it really start…not the beginning of two people's journey to the other side, but instead the pivotal moments in separate lives…separate places…each priming them to be in "the place" where they are meant to converge…to come together…the thread of a connection now growing taught.

Though we only recently came to find each other, our journey started long ago. "Our" story starts here, "27° 50' 2.0976" N and 97° 3' 39.9456"W

And so, the story shall be written as the journey moves forward, into time that we now share together. If these coordinates never existed, would we be holding hands now?
I loved you before we met, even if it was only in a dream. I love you more with every passing day. Take my hand, let's walk side by side with love in our hearts to the next chapter of life.

Bookmark - What if?

What if leaving what was familiar, instead was chasing a dream that we hadn't yet had?
11.19.2022

We were not allowed to meet each other until now, so we wouldn't hurt each other…for different reasons.

Any sooner and we would have missed the moment… a brief glimpse… eyes averted…missed… what would have been lost?

So many things had to be in place, the day, the hour, the circumstances, just so… to be ready in the moment of "what if"?

Bookmark – Hey

Hey Michelle
Yes John
Have I ever told you?
Told me what John…

There's something about you…so many something's…little something's…big somethings…all of those somethings that I love about you.
2.23.2023

Our layers of intimacy - what do they look like…feel like? It's not one thing, it's not 100 things…it's everything. As we talk about this, the MJ's…maybe it's the commitment, best rebooted each new day, with something as simple as the first cup of coffee…shared while still in bed…lest we forget that it's about the little things.

Morning Coffee

Our layers of intimacy - what do they look like…feel like? It's not one thing, it's not 100 things…it's everything. As we talk about this, the MJ's…maybe it's the commitment, best rebooted each new day, with something as simple as the first cup of coffee…shared while still in bed…lest we forget that it's about the little things.

Morning Coffee

Julieta Corpus

Julieta Corpus is a bilingual poet from Mexico. Her latest literary contribution is a collaboration with poet Katie Hoerth and visual artist Corinne Whittenmore: *Borderland Mujeres*, published by Texas A&M Press.

Her Cross To Bear

The beast beats up his wife
For no other reason, than to
Assert his manhood,
"I own you.
I could kill you if I wanted to."

She usually curls up in a corner
And closes her eyes.
She cannot fight back, even less so
When he's been drinking,
Alcohol increases his
Physical strength---fuels
The rage within.

He is the man of the house.
The lion in wait for any excuse
To pounce on her.
Lupe is only thirty years old,
But already her physical
Injuries trigger severe seizures.
And no matter how loud she
Screams, no one ever comes
To her rescue.

The neighbors simply shut
Their doors. Her family won't
Help, either. They warned her
Against marrying him.
But Lupe fell in love.

Now, her abusive husband is
"Her cross to bear."
His children are not spared
Any of the abuse, either.
All three boys have met
Every one of his demons.
He tries to bend the children
To his will with his belt buckle,
Boots, and fists.

Years later, he grows tired,
Leaves Lupe for another
Woman. He claims he's
Sick of her seizures, and her weeping,
"You're faking all of it. You're too weak."
The beast dies at seventy years
Old while crossing a busy
Street---heart attack. Guadalupe Escobedo, his wife,
My grandmother, outlived
Him by eight years.

Kimberly Ward

Icing Event

Lizbette Ocasio-Russe

Lizbette Ocasio-Russe is an Assistant Professor of English at TAMU-CC. This story, originally published in *Flash Fiction Magazine,* is about the aftermath of Hurricane María in Puerto Rico. Lizbette's short story collection *Loverbar* is available on Amazon and elsewhere.

María

I'd never seen her like that before. My baby girl's beautiful face was all twisted up in cruel realization. She stood with her trusted stuffed dog Chuito petrified like the wood María had scattered all over the street, the street she could no longer play on with her friends. Her friends . . . Many she didn't hear from for a month or two; others just kind of vanished. Whether it was the hurricane or the diaspora, I still don't know. She wouldn't speak; no matter how hard I tried to coax her out of silence, the blank stare and muteness remained. Not even the coconut candy I offered her cleared the fog stifling her consciousness. She was silent the whole time the storm raged, though the blankness had not arrived; only her wild eyes darting back and forth hinted at concern. Chuito never left her arms, though her grip on him loosened as the winds and rains roared into the morning. I'll never forget how the wind sounded gusting outside the rattling walls. It carried the voices of millions shrieking and crying across the island. It was thunder and lightning, explosions, crashes, and rock slides. I offered my baby girl some headphones and an old CD player to black out the chaos, but she refused.

"No. Quiero escuchar, Mami; I want to hear it," is all she said.

At first, what I perceived as bravery impressed me, but I would soon learn it wasn't just a matter of courage. When we finally came out of the closet, the tears were inevitable. Storm shutters blown away, windows broken, belongings gone or destroyed. Our pictures, all of our family photos, had either been carried away or ruined. Water damage, debris damage, psychological damage, emotional damage. It was everywhere you looked. The first to look outside was my baby girl. When I found her after assessing the damage to our home, she was standing where our front door used to be with Chuito hanging limply from her hand.

"Mi amor . . . sweetheart," I called to her. Nothing. "Everything is going to be okay," I assured her.

She dropped Chuito, his silent plush landing exterminating any hope I had managed to retain. María had taken my baby girl.

Louise Pettigrove

In her memoir, *Bright Fields,* Louise Knolle Pettigrove tells the story of her childhood on Knolle Jersey Farms, home of the World's largest Jersey Herd.

An excerpt from *Bright Fields*

Mollie Madray letter from 1891

Mathis, San Patricio Co.
Tex. May 29/91.

Mr Wallis Wade.

Friend Wallis:-

I received your most kind letter a few days ago. and you may imagine my surprise after contents were noted. I will now tell you what I think is best after a few days thought on the matter. I am not prepared to give you a final answer. owing to not being in your company much. we neither of us know the others disposition or ways for the few times we have met: but I think I have you down right. (which is the nicest young man I have met since I have

Nowadays, no one remembers anything about Wallis Wade's' first wife, Mollie Madray, except Mama. Now, three years after my visit to the Wade Ranch, I know more about her. She and Wallis wrote to each other while they were courting. Mollie's letters must have been saved by Wallis and then by Lou Ella. I'd found the letters in a satin envelope along with some old family photographs which had been given to me for safekeeping.

Mollie's fifteen letters tell the story of the growing intimacy between her and Wallis. In 1891, Mollie lived in Mathis with her family. At one of the dances, she'd gone to, she'd been voted "most popular girl." In May of that year, she received a letter from Wallis indicating his desire to marry her. She wrote back, "I propose waiting for several months, giving each time to know more about the other before entering into an engagement." They began to see each other frequently, usually at church, and they would correspond until the next Sunday or until they managed to meet again.

One of the barriers Wallis and Mollie encountered in their relationship was the Nueces River between them. It often flooded, and crossing it would've been impossible on horseback or with a horse and buggy. A ferry had been there since 1877, but it didn't run in bad weather. In September 1891, Mollie wrote, "So [I] guess you have had plenty of rain. We heard the river was up until today, so Joe and I would not start over to see you all: seems as if fate were against me getting over there.

After six months, Wallis was beginning to grow tired of the difficulties in seeing her, and he saw her apparent hesitation as another barrier. When he stopped answering her letters, Mollie began to worry about losing him. She sent a letter, saying:

> I've concluded to write and ask if you have forgotten my existence. Thought probably some other girl is ahead of me. And should [I] not wonder if there was? There being so many more attractive than poor little me. I do not wonder at your withdrawing your affections for you have certainly been sufficiently tried.

Their correspondence resumed. Mollie began to understand she was in love with Wallis when, at the conclusion of an argument between them, she'd noticed he was crying. "I did not realize how it would hurt you until you cried. I felt I knew you better than ever before." When Mollie realized how much she cared for him, she began to write more openly. On Christmas Eve, Mollie wrote, "I feel somehow as if you had found another girl. It ought not to make any difference with me, but I really do feel jealous. I sometimes think I care for you more than I thought I did."

In January of 1892, Mollie had finally made up her mind to marry

Wallis. She wrote, "If you have not forgotten what I promised the evening we went riding, come tomorrow week 'on Sunday', and I will tell you something, unless you have learned to care for some other girl, then of course I can't."

By February 9th, Mollie had given Wallis her answer, and she wrote to assure him:

> "Now Wallis, I have given you my promise, and don't you think for a moment I will break it." Then she turned to practical matters. "You spoke of having the marriage earlier than June! I can't promise to yet but may consent for it to be the latter part of April. . . . I have not yet mentioned anything to Mama or Papa or anyone. Will soon tell Mama."

Mollie's letters also tell of visits to friends and family, visits which often stretched into weeks. And now that Mollie was engaged, she became the object of teasing. "I think I will go home Tuesday or Wednesday. I have been having a very good time here ... They tried to tease me a little about you but were not at all successful."

In a letter written in March, Mollie explained about some comments from friends and relatives who had tried to influence her:

> Wallis, you do not blame me for answering you the way I did! Did you? I just tell you I did not know you enough to know my own mind, and I had a good deal to work against too: you have been told things on me and so have I on you. But I would not believe until I found out for myself. As to your talking, I have found out that the more I know you, the more you talk, true, you do not talk as much as most young men; but I am not afraid of your not talking enough. What you don't talk, I will make up for you.

Molly wasn't swayed by the gossip, and by March 19, she was counting the days until their marriage. But the biggest barrier of all, Mollie's health, soon became the couple's overriding concern. Her first mention of measles occurs in late March. Her poor health continued, and she died only months after the wedding. Wallis buried her in the Wade Cemetery on the Ranch where he would later be placed next to her. His second wife, Lou Ella, would be buried on his other side. Mollie's tombstone says simply:

Mollie Madray Wade
1868-1892

Today, that tombstone, half-covered by cactus, and the 15 love letters written in a clear flourishing hand are all I know that's left of Mollie Madray.

Lucas Jasso

Lucas Jasso graduated from McAllen High School in 1969. He enlisted in the U.S. Army and served in Viet Nam, earning Army Commendation medals and an Expeditionary Forces medal. He currently serves as a Master Trustee for the Texas Association of School Boards—and he writes.

Crabby

My granny brought clothes when I was a young tot. My mother bought clothes for me until I got married, and then my wife bought my clothes. That practice, by the three females in my life, made me develop anxiety. Returning from the Viet Nam War, the anxiety grew worse. In crowded places, I become hostile and intolerable. It's impossible to walk down crowded aisles where people brush against you. I become hotter than a stricken match.

One day, I had no choice but to buy provisions. Once inside the grocery store, I proceeded to the cereal aisle because I was out of my favorite delight for breakfast. A female in a motorized store cart blocked my path. Not wanting to go through the trouble of excusing myself and barely being able to maneuver around her anyway, I walked around to the opposite end.

Would you believe she had moved and stopped right in the path of my favorite cereal? She was busy gossiping with another squawking female. She noticed my flustered face, but she wouldn't move. I am not insensitive. However, there are inconsiderate people who will not use their common sense and decency to understand they are blocking the aisle.

When I walked to a different aisle, a young girl with purple hair asked, "May I help you find something?" I looked at her and said, "I'm interested in buying a coffin." She didn't quite know how to respond, staring with that wild amazed look.

I still have youthful mental agility. When people see me in a raincoat, they ask, "Oh, is it raining outside?" I say, "No, it is raining inside." When my neighbor says, "Climb down off of that tree," I say, "I think climbing refers to going up, not coming down." How about visiting a car dealership? "'Would you like to buy a car?" the salesman asks. "No, I want to polish it." Employment applications ask who to call in an emergency. I write, "An ambulance."

What is your reaction when losing your car keys? Do you look under the bed, sofa, pant pockets in laundry, in the automobile, in the freezer, and all over? After an exhausting hunting trip, you notice the jingle jangle in your pants pocket. Ugh!

Eventually you will reach a point when you stop lying about your age and start bragging about it. In high school I couldn't wait to turn twenty-one and be of drinking age. I did not get to enjoy it because I was drafted into the Army. Some people try to turn back their "odometers." Not me. I want people to know why I look this way. I've traveled a long way and a lot of the roads were not paved.

Mason Graves

Mason Graves was born in Corpus Christi and was raised almost all of his life here. After college, he hopes to pursue a career as a creative writer for video games

Thunder at Night

Dark sky, ripe with light

Drums from heaven sent to earth

A heart's desire

The Smell of Rain

A pitter patter

The smell of mud and ocean

Emptiness holds on

Why I'm Still Alive

I say, "It's bad today." She says, "I'm here."

Matthew Rosas

Matthew Rosas was born in Corpus Christi, TX. He is the author of The Legend of Mariquita and Other Short Stories, and of the recently released novella, Praying not to Fall.

Benjamin Sunrise

When not on the beach in the scorching hot Corpus Christi summers, my brother and I would ask my mother or my gramma Cita to drop us off at Sunrise Mall. In the mid-to-late late 80's, that place was like heaven for teens. We'd go to Aladdin's Castle for video games, head to Orange Julius for a cold drink, browse Camelot music to check out album covers, and drop by B Daltons to try to peek at a Playboy from the top shelf without getting caught.

The highlight of the visit, though, was always, always, Benjamin Surf & Sunwear. As we came up the escalator to the second floor, we could hear the catchy surf rock music, the kind even too cool for C101, and then see the brightly lit sign. BENJAMIN. Once inside, I'd first browse the shirts and shorts I couldn't afford, but loved to look at. My favorites were the Billabong. My brother liked Gotcha and Lightning Bolt. Then, I would move on to the T-Shirts and Benjamin always had the best. Every year for Christmas my mother would get me one and I would wear it only on special days. The girls who worked there would sometimes ask if I needed help, but I would shyly smile and shake my head because they were the prettiest girls that had ever spoken to me. If one approached, my teenage brain would dissolve into mush and my legs would almost give out. Next up, were the perfectly lined surfboards. Stussy and T&C were my favorites. I dreamed of owning a tri-fin and being able to surf like the pros. My dinged-up single fin 6'3" Surfboards Hawaii, bought used at Dockside, was the one and only board I'd ever used, but I cared for it like it a fancy new Cadillac. After looking at the boards, we would watch the TV with the latest VCR tapes playing surf videos. I could watch those for hours. You couldn't see this stuff on the 11 channels at home. The guys from the Surfing mags ripping it up at the most famous surf beaches. Tom Carrol, Mark Richards, Wayne Bartholomew, Shaun Tomson, Martin Potter, and big-wave warriors Gerry Lopez and Brad Gerlach. All legends. The best in my mind was Tom Curren. His drop-in, bottom-turn, and lightning-fast lip-whip could not be matched. He could read a wave better than all the others at that time. One more I loved to watch was Mark Occhilupo. Occy had wild hair, a loose style, and surfed with no fear.

Our last stop was the accessories and other items shelved near the register. I would grab a plastic bottle of Hawaiian Tropic sunscreen, flick the top open with my thumb, and smell the soothing coconut-scent. Then, on to the distinctively satisfying aroma of Mr. Zog's Sex Wax. I would pick a wax to take home, and my brother would usually pick either a wax or a sticker. We would head back down the escalator, find a pay phone to call for our ride, and on the way home I'd dream of a 6-foot drop-in, an epic tube-ride and a jammin' return trip to Benjamin.

Michael Quintana

Michael Quintana is a practicing writer that holds an MFA in Fiction and Screenwriting from San Jose State University. He currently works with writers and entrepreneurs through his company Script Journey for manuscript, speech, website, and brand and marketing development. To learn more about Script Journey, visit **www.scriptjourney.com.**
Michael's debut book of poetry *The Silence Holds Us Together* will be released in the Fall of 2023.

Two of Wands

Years from now
I want you to tell me
how I got that scar,
and how it felt to be so close to infinity.

The first time we went to Palm Springs,
just so you can show me Warhols
in the desert.

Weekend getaways, poolside,
times when I wondered
if this weekend would be the weekend
you'd crack us open like Goliath's skull

proving Didion right:
the center will not hold
and life does change in the ordinary instant.

Michelle Eccellente Stevenson

Michelle Eccellente Stevenson is an artist, writer, TEDx speaker, and founder of *Cultivate Caring*. The bulk of her career was spent in the training and development sector, working for major corporations as an educator. Michelle now spends her time trying to make sense of the world through art, writing, and content development. She invites you to join her on social media @CultivateCaring and @MESStudioArt.

Unlucky

The handwriting was on the wall from the start. Even my name, Mallory, is unlucky. My Mom saw it in a Teen Beat magazine and decided that day that if she had a girl, Mallory would be her name. As it turns out, Mallory is a nickname for the French word "malheure," meaning misfortune. Mom never looked up the meaning, and I don't think she would have changed her mind if she had.

I got a glimpse of lady luck's face in the fifth grade. My English teacher had us write a poem that we would then read out loud to the entire class. The topic was up to us. I procrastinated until the night before and wrote a really bad poem about my dog Scruffy. The day of the dreaded recitation, my teacher made us pick numbers out of a hat to determine the reading order. Prepubescent kids around me were starting to really sweat and it was even stinkier than normal. I wiped my own clammy palms on my pants and pulled out the number twenty-four, which meant I would be the last one to have to stand up and humiliate myself. Mercifully, the bell rang before it was my turn and that evening the teacher was struck by a black van and had to be hospitalized, so I never had to recite my terrible, embarrassing poem.

The only other time lady luck gave me a glance was on my twentieth birthday at the Goodwill store. Buying jeans was an ordeal. The waist is always too low and the length invariably too short for my almost six-foot frame. When I found ones that fit, I let out a little "woohoo!", thanking my lucky stars that I wouldn't have to pay full price somewhere else. Later that week, getting them ready to wash, I found twenty bucks in the back pocket. I felt like a real lucky-duck and figured I'd better not test that luck, so I put it in my car's glove compartment, reserved for "just in case" gas money. Since then, I haven't won any raffles, contests, never scratched off the right numbers, and never ever found money on the street.

I thought I recognized luck a few weeks ago when a friend set me up on a blind date. Turns out, thanks to the internet, blind dates aren't so blind anymore. I trolled him online and the pictures proved he was in fact tall, had a job, and hung out with his mom occasionally. A stand-up guy that was also easy-on-the-eyes. We talked on the phone a few times and finalized plans for the date. A full week before the meetup, he hadn't canceled yet. Lucky. Just this morning, he called and told me that he had to cancel because he got back together with his ex. Decidedly unlucky.

Not one to wallow in my all too familiar misfortune, I decided that luck be damned. I didn't need luck's insincere gifts and planned on going to the bookstore to spend that twenty bucks that had been sitting in my glove compartment. I put on my new-to-me jeans, threw on a light rain jacket, grabbed my bag, headed out the door, and retrieved the money from my parked car. A strong coffee, a walk in the cool air, and a new book was just what I needed. The used bookstore down the street had a good selection of sci-fi and a nutty, lightly caramelized latte that tasted like a holiday in the Alps. Perfect for getting my head back on straight.

Traffic was heavy but not more so than a normal day in the Emerald City. Drizzle collecting on my hair started to drip down my forehead and into my eyes so, I put my hood up. Stepping out into the crosswalk, I thought who needs luck anyway?

Me. That's who.

I heard the tires squeal behind me, turned left and saw the black van a second before it hit me, and the last thing I thought was damn, maybe I should have kept that twenty bucks in the glove compartment.

Mike Mercer

Mike Mercer has written two novels, *Forever Alone* and *The Blue Tequila Cantina.*

The Day I Learned I Could Never Live up to the Man!

So, it was late June 1957 in a half-harvested wheat field in the middle of God's Texas Panhandle. I was just turning 14. The heat fell heavy from the sky and was there to stay. The Dachshund was digging a hole under the pickup.

Gleaner Model A Combine sat idle with "frozen" 12-inch variable speed drive sheaves. The bearing on the shaft was still smoking.

Dad's 2-pound ball-peen hammer was driving a 12" coal chisel between the sheaves to loosen them on the shaft. Right side of the combine he was working on was in the bright almost-noon sunshine.

Stroke after stroke, the hammer pounded the chisel. After seeming hours of hammer on the steel, from behind the man, I misspoke, "Dad I don't think we are going to get the sheaves loose."

Dad missed two strokes with the ball-peen to say without anger, "these sheaves will come off," and began again swinging at the chisel.

In a while, I heard a strange sound like a spring releasing as the chisel left its place between the sheaves and traveled to dad's lower lip. Dad turned, took the red rag in my hand, and covered the cut just below his lip. He walked to the driver side mirror. Took a look, and I also saw the cut lip, and the roots of two lower front teeth looking back at us from the mirror. Dad stuck the rag in his mouth enough to slow the bleed.

Dad patted his leg twice, and Herb jumped to the floorboard then to the back of the seat as usual. Dad climbed aboard and we headed to the county road. Instead of turning toward town, we headed west. We drove in silence, but Herb leaned out past dad and barked at all passing vehicles.

In about an hour, we pulled up in front of Dr. Crawford dentist office Plainview Texas. With dog waiting under the truck, we entered the office. Receptionist wanted to know what's wrong, so dad showed her. In about 2 minutes, Dr. Crawford summoned dad to this chair behind closed doors.

One hour later, dad came out with a bandage on his lower lip and a bottle of pills. Motioned me with a let's go, and we headed to the truck. We and dog headed back the way we came. Looked like we were headed home. In about 45 minutes, we were about to pass the wheat field on our way home, but dad turned into the field. In five more minutes, dad was swinging the hammer striking the coal chisel. I readied the needed parts, fresh grease, a pan of gasoline to wash the sheaves and clean the parts we could re-use. I added a clean cloth to the assembled parts on the tailgate. I gave Herb a drink of water from the canvas water bag. Then I heard the outside sheave fall to the ground and the hammer was silent.

I saw a little blood on the bandage as dad cleaned, installed new bearings, and reassembled the sheaves on the combine. Lock washer and lock nut tightened; drive belts pried onto the sheaves. Dad smiled with his eyes and climbed the combine ladder and set the machine to harvesting wheat once again. It was almost dark but, I knew he would go till dew fell and stiffened the straw. Me and the dog rested, ready for the trip home. My dad had worn me out.

In a few weeks, the lip and the replanted teeth were looking pretty good. The man taught me another lesson about giving up, NEVER.

Sometimes I think he did all that just for me. Then I remember everything he did was just for me.

Jeff Janko

Woman on the Beach

Mona Schroeder

Mona Schroeder is a former librarian. This is an excerpt from her novel, *Random Acts.*

Honey

"Honey, no offense," Meryl said, touching Cecilia's arm across the table, "but you really need to get hold of yourself. You can't let this thing with your husband get you down. Sometimes men get these crazy ideas in their heads. Charles thinks he's in love with a woman I'm not even sure is real. Frankly, I suspect she's a mannequin."

"A mannequin?" Cecilia stared at her.

"Or maybe one of those Japanese sex robots. They're very realistic. It's no wonder Charles was fooled." Meryl raised her eyebrows dramatically.

"Have you met her?"

"Yes! The woman is crazy thin. It's almost scary. She makes Kate Moss look like Roseanne. And she has this weird, poreless skin. It's hard to tell how old she is. She may be older than I am for all I know. Wouldn't that be a hoot?" She laughed and took another bite of cake. "Who's your guy shacking up with?"

"I'm not sure."

"Not sure? Well, we have to do some recon and find out then. You have to know who the enemy is. That's the first principle of war. I have a brunette wig you could borrow."

"I don't think so, Meryl."

"It's no trouble. I have to do my rounds at Charles's new house anyway to see what he's up to. We can swing by your husband's place on the way."

"No, thanks. Really."

"Well, what say we go over to the mall, then? What you need is a make-over."

Under the harsh glare of the sunlight, Meryl's makeup looked garish, and her hair looked unnatural, almost like a Q-tip. It was too much, Cecilia thought . . . the blush, the purple eye shadow, and the heavy eyeliner. She could see where the foundation had collected in the tiny creases under Meryl's eyes. She stared at her without meaning to and pitied her desperate attempt to find herself in hair dye and over-done makeup. And then, as she looked at Meryl, she realized she was just trying to survive. They both were . . . and sometimes you did have to expose yourself in a way to other people. There was no way to stay insulated all the time, no matter how attractive that idea sometimes seemed.

"My son died," Cecilia said, and then wondered if she had actually said the words aloud or merely thought them.

Jen Deselms

Surfer under Horace Caldwell Pier

Neesy Tompkins

Neesy Tompkins writes about Port Aransas, particularly "Old Port A." She has 43,000 Facebook followers, and this Facebook post received two thousand likes and thirteen shares.

Shorty's

Under a big Texas Sky and a waxing moon in Sagittarius, Shorty's, in preparation of being moved.

It is moving, emotionally, just to look at it now. An old iconic legend where new concrete parking lots have surrounded and replaced old oyster shells, and newer buildings with shiny paint have crowded near this old bar and her crumbling exterior, the antiquity of pilings used as a foundation.

It is moving, emotionally, just looking at it and the memories it houses. Old dusty baseball caps, signed by their owners and left to adorn the ceiling. A memory in time. But, it is Ms. Rose whose memory sits on that last bar stool at the end, with her twinkling blue eyes; her old pig collection in memory of all those pig parties. Those old creaky wood floors can never be replaced, nor the view from the ladies room facing the harbor at sunset, or the old fashioned jukebox with Larry Joe Taylor singing his Texas Coastal music.

Like a story fresh out of a Faulkner novel, this Rose, our Ms. Rose, maintained the family business the duration of her life even as the face of Port Aransas changed all around her, this old building inherited from her Mom. But nothing can ever replace all the memories contained within these saturated walls.

Pretty sure there's probably some long lost wedding rings and old coins, maybe even a bullet or two underneath that building.

Old timers tell of a time when gambling was frequent there, and when the ferry boat captain would call to warn of incoming coppers, the money quickly thrown into old wooden coca cola 12 pack cases and moved out the door.

If these walls could talk, the story they would tell. An end of an era. Edwin Myers is now the owner of Shorty's and while still unclear as to why Shorty's is being moved, one thing is for sure - the flats will never be the same. To care enough about old historic buildings and this old bar, keeping the building alive, in this time in Port Aransas is a rare thing. Hopefully, onward to a new location that will prosper, though uprooted, for another 100 years.

For now, a waxing moon symbolizing the end of things, shining her glow upon what might be Shorty's last night at this home of hers for so many years, twinkling like the eyes of Ms. Rose, as if she is still here, watching over her old bar. Man, if these walls could talk......

William Mays

Water Snake

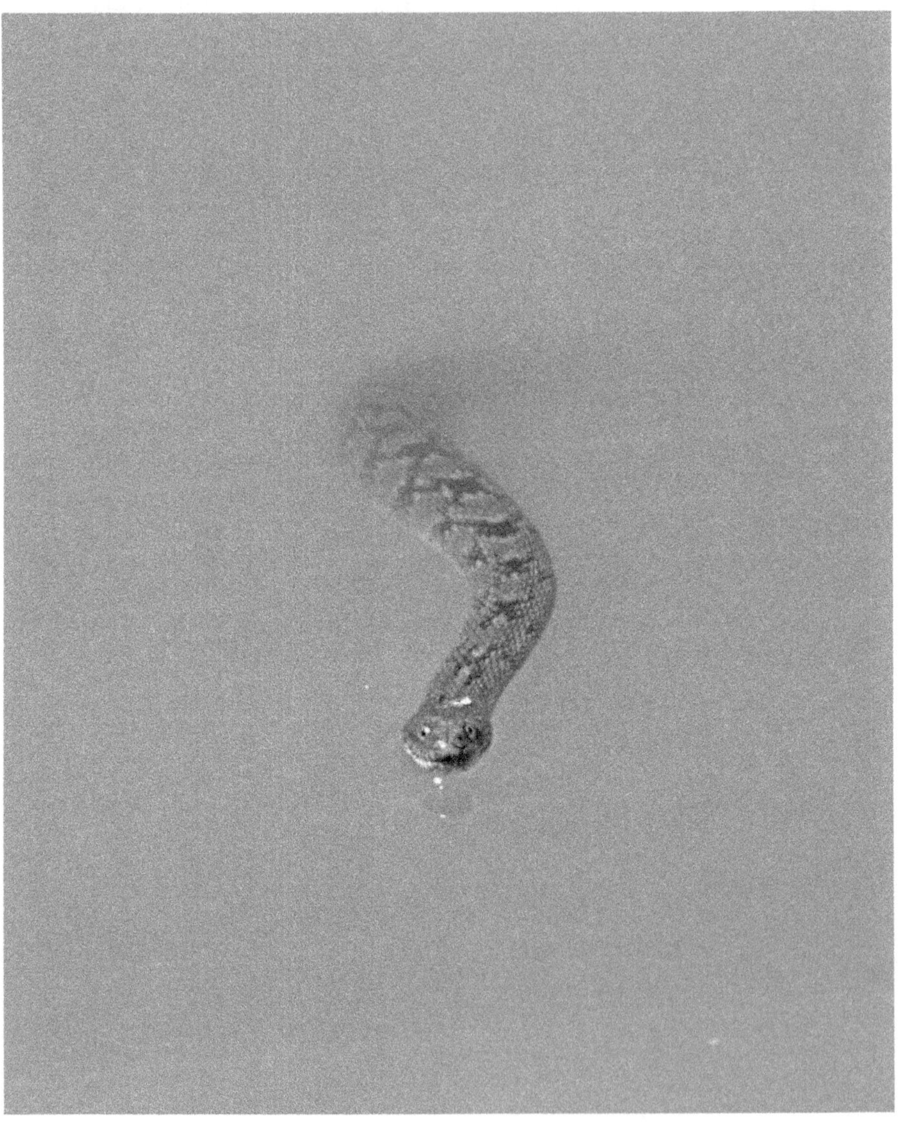

Neina Chapa

Neina is a biologist who embraces her artistic side when she needs a break from reading scientific articles and data analysis. This is the first time she has let anyone besides close friends read her poetry.

The Snake Escape

We used to slither through the marsh
Peek out under brush and burrow in soft karst
Nestle in between the bark and heart of a warm tree
Waiting till we can bask in the sun's warm decree
Cold-blooded but hot with desire
We knew not of what was soon to transpire
We would glide underwater and snag our piscivorous prey with a snap
Bellies bulging from the nutrients as the meal fought back with a flap
One evening on our nocturnal hunt, we saw a shimmery gleam
What a fortuitous night as our frames had been turning lean
We slinked through the hole like it was made just for us
And gorged on terrorized fish till we could almost bust
At last we licked our scaled lips and ventured to leave late
Only to find the hole was as sealed as our fate
Our slit eyes in panic as we sought out each other
In this watery world we were doomed to suffer
We were left to consider how it all went wrong
Missing the place where we belong
And in the next early light we heard a low rumble
A murderous machine wheeling along with a grumble
We thrashed and rubbed snouts on the wire mesh
Trying to find the place where it gives and not stopping to rest
Suddenly the cage was heaved from the water and we sizzled in the sun
Predators in boots keenly eyed us, and we thought we were done
They unlatched the door and gave our prison a shake
Out we flopped on the limestone like the fish we ate
Made to feel like we were discarded
Our love soon darkened

And we could focus on nothing but our quick escape
Unaware of the rift in passion it would create
With every muscle engaged our adrenaline pushed us to slither
Forked tongues flicker, we should have fled together under the nearby leaf litter

But we sought refuge in opposite hideouts and became separated forever

Lu Ann Kingsbury

Corpus Christi Bayfront

Octavio Quintanila

Octavio Quintanilla is the author of the poetry collection, *If I Go Missing*, the founder and director of the literature & arts festival, VersoFrontera, publisher of Alabrava Press, and former Poet Laureate of San Antonio, TX. He teaches Literature and Creative Writing at Our Lady of the Lake University. Connect on IG: @writeroctavioquintanilla

Abstract Borderland 93

Octavio Quintanilla calls his visual poetry "Frontextos," a portmanteau of the Spanish word, "Frontera" and "Texto" (Border/Text). Since 2018, he has published daily Frontexto on his social media. At first, the text was usually accompanied by a black and white image sketched (usually) on a Moleskin 3.5" x 5.5"; however, the complexity of the Frontextos has been expanding and transforming as he learned new ways to make them and as he researched and dialogued with different traditions of visual poetry such as object poetry, lettrism, asemic writing, concrete poetry, illuminated manuscripts, calligrams, etc.

Abstract Borderland 166

Pete Adler

Originally from West Virginia, Pete Adler has spent the past 49 years in Corpus Christi. He compiles "found poems" with each line taken from an internet news site headline.

Greased Tea

floating downriver on a stolen Ouija board
carrying only a rucksack filled with unspoken prayers
    and empty dreams.
he took my life and I didn't mind.

later found in a ratty pool hall
somewhere in Burbank
hustling at snooker and darts
    back when Craig Kilborn was a thing

migrating from silks and satins to
    earthy cardigans
    grandad wore in the early spring,
reclusive, prolific
  the veneer was fading
  tongues were wagging
    the die-hards could never understand.

I saw him on the old Zenith once
as a lion tamer in a Brylcreme commercial
    or was it a hair restoration ad?
he looked happily bored
    no regard for your opinion, no opinion of your regard.
how soon is now; how long ago then?
speak ill of the near dead and they will haunt your closets
    and turn the roses black.

Pete Lutz

Pete Lutz is a native of Illinois and a U.S. Navy retiree who finished his military career in South Texas and decided to stay. A lover of and writer of poetry since youth, Pete claims as his chief inspirations Dr. Seuss, James Whitcomb Riley and Ogden Nash. He is the creator of several audio drama series, and a collection of his scripts was just published this year.

RADIOACTIVE RON, a Tale of an Apocalypse
A Crown of Sonnets

Suggested by Juan Manuel Perez

"Radioactive Ron is on the air,
With tunes to make you wanna twitch your hips;
And some designed to make you sit and stare,
And contemplate this new apocalypse."
I say this ev'ry day as I sign on,
Repeat it sev'ral times in case they hear:
For survivors, are there any? Patty? John?
Family, friends? Or strangers, far or near?
And in-between I broadcast every song
That I can get my hands on, jazz or rock,
Hip-hop, R-and-B, plus Muni Long,
Or William Haley's "Rock Around the Clock".
    Music doesn't matter; message does:
    To wit: Earth ain't the place she used to was.

To wit: Earth ain't the place she used to was,
And everything just happened all at once –
One day your baby's face is soft as fuzz,
The next he's tatted up and smoking blunts.
Don't ask me why, I'm up here all alone:
The twenty-seventh level is my lair.
There's no one left to call me on the phone,
Or join me, sitting in that other chair.
We're getting power, no one sends a bill –
How long we'll have it, only heaven knows.
And thus the empty hours do I fill,
Like the emp'ror, my purpose has no clothes.
    But naked though it be, what helps me cope?
    That thing with feathers, Emily's friend, hope.

That thing with feathers, Emily's friend, hope
Sustained me in the early days of this,
When I was strung out, feeling like a dope
And standing 'bout an inch from the abyss.
I screamed, I cried, I called out ev'ry name
Of ev'ryone I'd seen the day before:
My wife, my kids, my friends! And then my shame
At stealing unpaid items from a store;
But hope soon drew me backward from the ledge.
I reasoned that there couldn't be just me;
So in my heart I made a tearful pledge:
My fellow humans, where'er you may be,
    Find you I duly must, I told myself.
    I took determination off the shelf.

I took determination off the shelf,
And like a shawl upon my shoulders wear;
I'm sending out my words, up north of Guelph,
And south of Rio, bouncing on the air.
For entertainment's sake, my voice ain't much,
And these old records really show their age.
If you hear me, I hope you'll get in touch –
But zombies, please just shuffle past my cage.
Although, to tell the truth, I think I might
Be glad to see the stumbling undead pass;
See something moving, other than the light,
Or the wind as it shifts the dying grass.
    It doesn't really change much here, the view:
    It's nice enough, but better seen by two.

It's nice enough, but better seen by two,
And by now, I'm not picky – I don't care -
Male or female, dog or pony, kangaroo –
All free to join me in that other chair.
It serves me, usually, to act aloof:
To act as if I wouldn't even glance
At another living being's foot, or hoof –
'Blivious as Joe Cool at his school dance.
It's always quiet, but even more at night,
And at these times aloofness goes bye-bye:
Emotion swallows me – my throat grows tight,
And saved-up lonesome tears for hours I cry.
    'Til I emerge next morning, hoarse, and spent:

Another day to shine and represent.

"Another day to shine and represent!"
I tell myself each morning as I choose
The records that would make me president
If tunes were votes instead of rock and blues.
I represent mankind in glory full:
"Today, no war!" ironically I shout;
"Peace prevails!" My symbol is a gull:
Unfortunately, doves have all died out.
From my tower I can see an unmanned tank,
Empty Humvees, big guns topside-mount;
But Generals and Colonels I outrank:
My "Last Man Standing" status? Don't discount.
I flip a switch – into the mic I stare:
"Radioactive Ron is on the air!"

"Radioactive Ron is on the air!"
That house is empty, no one dwells within.
"Radioactive Ron is on the air!"
School is vacant, no class to begin.
"Radioactive Ron is on the air!"
Corner store is free of shoppers now.
"Radioactive Ron is on the air!"
Stock market has stopped ticking off the Dow.
"Radioactive Ron is on the air!"
Fields overgrown with sticker-burrs and weeds.
"Radioactive Ron is on the air!"
Libraries full of books that no one reads.
"Hey, humanity! Is anybody there?
Radioactive Ron is on the air..."

Roberta Dohse

Roberta Shellum Dohse graduated from the University of California, Berkeley. She spent time on a farm in Northern Minnesota and in Oregon. She moved to Texas and practiced law for many years. She always loved to write.

My Mother's Hands

My hands have become
Those of my mother
As they stretched over the piano keys
Reaching to correct a missed note,
As she bent close over the dress
With needle and thread
To stitch the finest hem.

As I knead the bread, I look down
To see her hands as they gently cradle
The beautiful orchids, pride and joy of the garden.
And I wonder if the same hands
Helped Grandma churn the butter,
Weed the mustard from the alfalfa,
Milk the cows.

How far we have come
To have orchids grace our lives,
Their sweet presence filling the room
As those hands brushed my hair.
Her ring now rests lightly on my finger,
Light as a kiss from heaven,
And I feel her press my hands in hers.

Watercolor Days

I still think of you and wonder what you are doing now,
though the winds of time have blown us onto different paths.
The times we had were magical, set apart,
when I was the center of your world.

When I look back I see only you and me,
watercolor days, golden ripples melting time and space,
your smile, your face, softened now in memory's glow
as when we were the only ones we knew.

Nature's gift enfolded us in a silent world of white,
ice sculptured trees sparkled in the morning light
and music breathed in and out of every thought
when you held me captured in your heart.

Your laughter and soft touches, they still warm my soul
as if you are still with me now to see this day,
to share the space between the moments once again,
as when you were the center of my world.

Foggy Days

I once lived in a small studio
with a large bay window
that didn't look onto anything,
other into a small barren courtyard
in the middle of the building.
But I could see the sky
and open the windows and take the air.
That was where I put my bed,
and my blue and white café curtains
with which I was quite pleased.
I had my desk, a very small chair,
my bookshelves and my books. Many books.

My studio was across the hall
from the stairs that led up to the roof
and there I would take in the whole of the city.
The lush gardens and old trees to the north
surrounding the Palace of Legion of Honor
where Rodin's statues held court.
I thought of him often.
And further on, just the tip of the golden bridge.

From the west, fresh salt air drifted
up from Land's End,
bringing, sometimes, the rolling fog
that blanketed everything in mystery,
muffling all sounds.
I would lift my chin, feel the damp air
kiss my skin, and soak in the distant roar of surf,
the ethereal calls of fog horns
as ships crept in through the gate.
And I wondered why
these seemed such lonely sounds to me.

Robin Carstensen

Robin Carstensen is the Coordinator of the Creative Writing Program at TAMU-CC where she advises *The Windward Review*, literary journal of the South Texas Coastal Bend. She is also senior editor for *The Switchback Review*. She is the 2023-2024 Poet Laureate of Corpus Christi.

Zoonoses

You could feel the stern
of your childhood
strike a sharp edge,

listing, when you heard
the velvet
flapping

camp of bats
dislodged,
sound-echoing

in their night flight, you could
hear the stern crack
open an eye

of a needle
you could see through
to the starched field

the bats left after the cows
were ushered in
beyond the field you could hear

a cow's long grazing moan
in Oklahoma, brown-pink
snout,

pink sow too,
muzzle-deep, rich
deep soil and pure lake

of her
eyes, *blessings*
of earth on the sow . . .

from the fodder and slops
to the spiritual
curl of the tail . . .

when you see the video
gone viral
of the quick pits,

deep
trenches
pitched

sounds
scratching
air

high smoke
skies stacked
to the burnt ground,

when you heard
pink shocked mouths,
a thousand

and a thousand more
down to the great
broken heart,

you could hear your stern
split into a million
treble peals

that could bring nothing, save
nothing, offer nothing
but a *spurting*

shuddering
maw

still suckling
gods
you can’t see.

after Galway Kinnell

*first published in *EcoTheo Review (Spring 2022)*

Roy Gomez

Roy Gomez earned an AA in English from Del Mar College in Corpus Christi, Texas, and is currently working on a BA in English at Texas A&M-Corpus Christi. He recently sat on the Short Prose Forms Panel at the 8th Annual Peoples Poetry Festival. Roy Gomez lives with his wife, two kids, and far too many cats.

A Change Is Coming

Alan's suicide note was delivered Priority Express in a sky-blue Hallmark envelope. What a brazenly final move! He must have dropped it in the mailbox with no reservations about his intentions. There was no return address, but I recognized his graffiti style handwriting. I struggled to find the courage to open it. Several months had elapsed, and yet, the regret and desire for absolution had not dissipated since our final interaction.

Our relationship was one sided. The only way he could get me to spend time with him was to show up at the low-traffic record store I work at. He committed my schedule to memory. As a result, I spent my days pleading with the seconds; hoping he wouldn't show up and hold me hostage until the end of my shift. He was ten years my junior, seven inches shorter than me, and always yapping away like a chihuahua when in familiar company. He was the little brother of a friend of mine, and somewhere along the way he got the impression that we were close friends. He even gave me a switchblade adorned with an image of the Virgin Mary against the backdrop of the Mexican flag.

Alan suffered from what I believed were delusions of grandeur. He would often begin conversations with "I almost had to kick some dude's ass the other day!" or, "I almost got into some shit this weekend at Chuck E. Cheese!" And no matter what story I told him; he always felt the need to one-up me. I once expressed relief after finishing a poem that I had trouble with, and he said, "You should have told me. You're never going to believe this, but when I was in high school, I won a poetry contest for a poem I wrote about getting arrested when I was 12." That was his favorite over-used idiom, "You're never going to believe this, but..." Another time, I told him about these two little girls from down the street who I caught throwing eggs at my house. Alan responded by saying, "You're never going to believe this, but one time I had to pull my gun on a guy that kept stealing my mail." There was always some fantastical lie to self-aggrandize his legacy.

Not all of his visits were focused on how he "kept it real."

Sometimes he sought me out to vent. He would get really deep—sometimes on the verge of tears. He would tell me about his prior anger issues and current loneliness, but he always assured me he was doing well. Although annoyed, I would do my best to give him advice, while also thinking, *I'm at work.* This low-level job does not pay me enough to be a therapist. I have my own problems. For years I allowed this to continue. I wanted to be honest with him, but he always seemed too fragile to take rejection.

Alan's estranged mother abandoned the family when he was a baby, and his father passed away a few years after. He told me he was raised by his uncle—a weed dealer named Oracio. According to Alan, Oracio had a Sulphur-crested cockatoo named Chancho who always sat perched on his uncle's shoulder. Supposedly, Chancho wore a tiny gold chain around his neck to match the larger one worn by Oracio.

After Alan's wife left him, he repeatedly boasted about Abbey and Mary. He referred to them degradingly as the "two fine honeys" who vied for his affection. I could not fathom a world in which my friend—quiet, scrawny little Alan—was stringing along two girls at once, but I always figured the fractured relationship with his mother caused him to make up stories about the women in his life.

Apparently, Alan was also a brown belt in Ju Jitsu. I found this the most ridiculous of his stories. He often spoke about training young martial arts students. He fancied himself a mentor to troubled children and told stories about changing lives and molding minds, as if he was Jaime Escalante from *Stand and Deliver*. I often wondered if he kept a rolodex or an excel spreadsheet to keep track of all these lies.

The last time I saw Alan, the sun was setting on a difficult day filled with school, work, and on top of all of it, fear of his spontaneous entrance. I was alphabetizing the "New Arrivals" while listening to a "Sounds of the 60's" playlist on the in-house speakers when I heard the chime from the ADT security system.

He didn't start with his usual, "What Up?" stuff. Instead, he looked really sad. "I'm in a bad place," he said. I must have made a face because he stopped and asked me what was wrong. In the silence that followed, the opening strings to Sam Cooke's "A Change is Gonna Come" began to play over the in-house speakers. In that moment, I was overcome with an overwhelming need to finally be honest with Alan. I was tired of him coming into the store whenever he pleased and spending hours on end reminiscing about events I didn't remember, or the stories about his hood mentality, his mentorships, and the females he was romancing. I tried so hard to stop myself. The owl on the cover of Rush's *Fly by Night* album, the children on Led Zeppelin's *Houses of the Holy*, and all four Beatles crossing *Abbey Road* seemed to be staring at me from the bins like, "Don't do it, man." But like magma pushed up from vents and fissures deep within the earth—I erupted.

"So? I know it's slow here, but I'm at work. Do you understand? It may not be busy, but I still have things I need to do. I don't have time to hear you tell stories about things I don't remember or lies about these fights you seem to always almost get into. I literally live in terror by the chance that you might come in here to visit with me. Listen, I love you, man; you're a good kid, but I'm not your therapist; I'm not your mom. I'm not your fucking dead dad, so please stop trying to replace him with me."

I'll never forget the tears welling up in his eyes, his face red and rapid breathing. He nodded, turned around and walked out of the store. I picked up a nearby pricing gun and threw it against the brick wall; it exploded into pieces and its small plastic parts fell to the floor making a tinny sound like Lego's hitting concrete. I marched towards the back office to sit down, visibly shaking from the adrenaline and shame of what I had just done. Whenever this memory creeps into my head, I scream as if I could somehow yell it out of my skull.

The funeral service was way across town. Alan had moved to that part of town years ago. The place was packed, and I didn't know anybody there. I felt I had traveled into an exotic corner; a foreign part of an otherwise familiar area.

Holding back regret, I floated down the maroon carpeted aisle up to his casket and kneeled. My shame extended beyond the pulpit and altar, beyond the vaulted ceiling and steeple, beyond this plane of existence and the next. In the casket lay a stranger. The absolute stillness of his body was like the eerie aftermath of a hurricane. I realized that most people are mysteries. In that moment, I realized I was never mad at him, but insecure about myself. I was mad about all his lies because they were proof that maybe I wasn't living, but rather watching my life pass me by.

As I turned to walk away, I noticed one of the portraits set up to the right of his casket. It was my friend Alan, bowing towards the camera, dressed in a Ju Jitsu Gi—brown belt, of course. The pew in front of the portrait was filled with young kids with somber faces, clearly mourning their lost mentor. Across the aisle, also in the front row, were two woman I had never seen. Both dressed in black, crying, and wearing funeral veils. One had on a necklace with a charm that read, "Abbey." I could only assume that the other woman was Maria. The fog surrounding Alan's lies began to dissipate into truths. And of course, sitting in the back was a man wearing a cowboy hat, gold chain, black silk shirt, blue jeans, and boots. A Sulphur-Crested cockatoo was perched on his shoulder—gold chain included. I quietly introduced myself. Oracio said he knew who I was; Alan had spoken fondly of me. He asked how I was doing; Alan had mentioned that I always seemed sad.

One by one, attendees stood behind the pulpit and spoke beautifully about how Alan had positively affected their lives. They spoke of the children he helped, the donations he'd made. His Ju Jitsu coach even made light-hearted jokes about having to calm Alan down when he would get into little scraps all around town. "He demanded respect," the coach said, "and he wasn't afraid to check someone for stepping out of line."

On my drive home, I thought about how selfish I had been. Turns out I didn't know Alan at all. He wouldn't come visit me because he was lonely or because he needed to build himself up. He did it to help me. He must have seen the pain inside of me that he thought he could alleviate by offering me the company of an old friend. He could see the pain through my silence. Sometimes those who are hurting are the ones most willing to help when they see the pain they feel inside someone else.

I used the switchblade Alan had given me as a letter opener. I dragged the edge of the blade against the sky-blue Hallmark envelope and unfolded Alan's last words to me. He opened the body of the letter with a humorous observation that only Alan could pull off. It said: "You're never going to believe this but—I'm dead!"

He wasn't lying. He's gone now, and I'm never going to believe it.

Sarah K. Lenz

Sarah K. Lenz is the author of the essay collection, *What Will Outlast Me?* (Unsolicited Press, 2023). Her creative nonfiction has appeared in *Colorado Review, New Letters, Triquarterly,* and elsewhere. Her work has been named Notable in *Best American Essay* three times. Sarah is an Assistant Professor of English at Del Mar College. She writes the newsletter, *Spirit: Notes for the Creative Contemplative*
Follow her at **https://sarahklenz.substack.com/**.

Excerpt from Code Grenadine

When a glass shatters in a restaurant in or near the beverage station's ice bin, the employee closest quickly douses the whole bin with Grenadine, that pomegranate mixer that's the essential ingredient in a Shirley Temple. The squirts of vermillion syrup, splashed like a horror film slayer scene alerted every one of the danger. Don't touch.

I worked in restaurants throughout most of undergrad and grad school, and being part of the service industry was such a formative experience that I often have flashbacks like this. Whenever a Code Grenadine happened, almost always during a rush, I was amazed by the swiftness the danger was dealt with. We worked together, FAST, to fix the problem because if we didn't, beverage service would grind to a halt and everyone would suffer a loss in tips. Whoever was able: bartender, manager, server, food runner, or busser, all hands on deck, formed a bucket brigade. First, gallons of boiling water, enough to melt 6 cubic feet of ice, then a thorough cleaning to remove all the glass, then the refilling of the ice bin requiring multiple trips with 20-pound buckets of ice, scooped from the machine in the back of the house. This was a tremendous amount of labor.

Those moments when we were all working together to hold our shit together, well, I tell you, that they felt really special. Collectively we all had a stake in getting the ice bin back and running, making sure the customer didn't even notice anything had gone wrong, and that no one got a glass-shard spiked drink. Under normal circumstances, we'd trash talk each other, and prank each other, and fight over side work assignments, but during a Code Grenadine, I never heard anyone berate someone for breaking a glass. It was such a big mistake, and one that was such pure accident, that the unstated rule was the culprit felt shitty enough about it and didn't need anyone getting all up in their business about it. It was a grace we gave each other.

Once a glass shattered in my hand over an ice bin and cut myself so badly I had to go to urgent care and get stitches, but the second that

Grenadine splashed on the ice, my co-workers had my back. They leapt into action to solve the problem my messy accident caused.

In the restaurants I worked at, there was no blaming when the glass shatters, no yelling, because that will only escalate the problem, and if there's crying, well it's best done in private, in the walk-in cooler. It's more time-efficient than going to the employee restroom to cry.

Scott Wayland Griffin

Lately, Scott Wayland Griffin has been teaching bush-crafting and outdoor survival techniques when he's not traveling with his two miniature dire wolves (Siberian Huskies)

The First Wolf

The days grew longer; snow melted; life slowly returned to the valley. The pups were finally allowed to venture out to play.

Moshadoe joined in the fun, it all came so easy to him. He was better at play fighting and stronger than the others. There was something more to it though, for he was able to use strategy and could also tell what the other pups were going to try before they knew it themselves.

Soon he grew bored with all the biting and wrestling. He wandered away from the group and followed a narrow path through the new grass and patches of snow. The yipping sounds coming from the den area grew faint behind him as he continued along the worn trail, letting it lead him down the hillside and into the dark forest. He felt a sense of pride with himself, none of the other pups would be brave enough to venture this far. He was enjoying the new smells that the forest offered as he leaped and hopped over gnarled tree roots and fallen branches.

As he rounded a bend in the path, he stopped suddenly in wonder.

It was his first time to see a river and he wasn't too sure what to make of it. The dark water gurgled as it coursed over rocks and it made lapping sounds against its banks. He took a few tentative steps towards it, determined to figure out just what it was.

He jumped out of his fur when a gruff voice from behind him spoke. "You should not be here, young one!"

Moshadoe turned and let out a sigh of relief as he recognized old Varoun, the best hunter in the pack.

"Why not? asked the pup, his eyes full of innocence.

"Because it's not allowed, pups must stay close to the den. It's always been this way."

"Always?" asked Moshadoe.

Varoun thought on this and replied, "Yes, always. Ever since the time of the first wolf."

He smiled at his own cleverness, surely this pup couldn't argue with something that has been a rule for that long. He was at a complete loss for an answer when Moshadoe asked him in a rapid manner,

"Who was the first wolf? What was his name? Where did he come from? What color was his fur? Did we all come from this one wolf? Why are some wolves white or brown or black?"

As he asked each question, he stepped closer to Varoun, who was caught so off guard that he began backing up with each step the pup took towards him. Finally, he could retreat no further, as he'd backed himself up against a tree.

"Enough, enough, I don't have all the answers." Then he quickly added, "Umm, go ask your mother."

Moshadoe followed Varoun back to the den, unhappily. Later, when he asked his mother the very same questions, she wasn't able to give him any answers either.

He stayed up late that night, thinking very hard on these matters concerning where the first wolf came from. He had asked all the adult wolves but didnt really get any answers that satisfied him. The reason he could get no answers was that none of the adults had ever wondered about this before and they each figured that one of the pack probably knew, but they didn't want to admit not knowing the answer themselves.

By the time he drifted off to sleep, he had made up his own answers.

The next evening he decided to share his tale with the other pups. They were full from eating and feeling very lazy, so they listened to him. Some of the adults nearby lifted their heads and cocked their ears to hear what this meddlesome pup was saying. They had all suffered his questions and now they were curious to hear what he may have learned from each other about the first wolf. In time, it became the story all the wolves were to teach their young..........

> The very first wolf was called Arue. She came to the world when all was new and the land was filled only with animals that ate the grass. She came down from the moon and saw that this valley was dying. There were too many deer & rabbits & mice. They fought with each other for the grass that they eat.
>
> The sun helps plants to grow but there were just too many animals. Soon there would be no grass left and they would all die. So Arue called to her mate, Gurrah. He came down to her from the sun and they thought about what to do.
>
> Arue said, "Let's kill and eat some of these animals so that the rest will live." Gurrah agreed and so they began to hunt. They were very big, but it took them a long time to eat enough of the deer, rabbits
>
> They ate and ate and ate but when they were full they saw that there were still too many animals.

"We need more help," said Arue, but Gurrah was tired and said he was leaving. He jumped up into the sun to watch, but would help no more.

So, she made more wolves from whatever she could find. She used snow to make white wolves, and the bark from trees to make brown ones. Then Arue used the black earth to make black wolves, and from boulders, crushed beneath her mighty paws, gray wolves.

She made many wolves, enough for several packs but they were still just lumps of snow, bark, earth and rock, they needed life.

Arue called to Gurrah and he finally agreed to give life to the wolves, for the sun gives life to all things.

Arue taught them to hunt and everything else we know today.

Then they divided into the packs to live in different ends of the valley, agreeing to come back here each spring to choose new mates. Each pack looked to Arue, thinking she would go with them, but she howled a long, lonely song, telling the wolves to hunt well and to remember her. Then faster than any normal wolf can move, she turned away and climbed the highest rock. She looked down at the packs below and then leapt into the night sky. She jumped very high, back to her home, back to the moon where she lives.

Every wolf was sad that she left and they called to her over and over but she didn't come back. Each night that the wolves hunted, they would call to Arue, the mother of all wolves, in hopes that she would come back. She never did, but we still call to her before we hunt at night. Maybe she will be watching and will be happy knowing that we are hunting the way she taught us. Maybe some night she will return.

When he finished his tale, the other wolves stared in amazement. They could see no reason to doubt his word. When the other pups fell asleep and the adults were leaving to hunt, Moshadoe stood in the entrance of their den watching and listening as the pack moved off in search of game. He heard them whispering...

"Yes, that was a very interesting story he made up," Varoun said. "He did make it all up himself, didn't he?

Garoun cast a look back at the pup, then looked to the moon

hanging full in the night sky.

"I don't know, my brother. It was a very good tale though."

Then both Garoun & Varoun lifted their muzzles and began the song of the pack.

"We sing to the wind in the trees.
We sing to the moon that guides our way home.
We sing to the sun that warms the earth and brings life.
All things must die. We will die too, but not today."

Margaret Cleaves

Little Tallapoosa Park, Georgia

Sophia Chapa

Sophia Chapa is a high school student who paints and writes to express her opinions and emotions. Creative writing has been life changing.

The Ocean

It's so calm and still
As I drive by in the mornings
I see how beautifully calm it is.
A part of me wishes I was that calm
I wish I can be calm and go with the flow
Not an anxious ball of mess.
But hey,
Isn't the ocean like that too?
Even though it's calm in the mornings
At night the waves become loud with a
hard crash like the cries I have at night
But
I'm still jealous of the ocean because
The ocean is calm.

Night time

I sit outside, trying to focus on myself.
Not the chaos around me.
Not the cars honking and zooming by.
And not the bright city lights that light up the night sky.
Instead when I am outside, in the night,
I can only hear the sounds of the wind
I can only feel the wind hit the skin of my face and body.
As the wind hugs me, I feel a welcoming feeling.
A feeling that never gets old.
It's a feeling that nature knows I'm reaching out.
and so I listen to the wind
because the wind guides me in the right direction of the night.

Cynthia Giery

Stranded on Padre Island

Stephen Gambill

Originally from Abilene, Steven Gambill eventually found his way to Corpus Christi. He considers himself a spiritual seeker in the Christian and Sufi mystical traditions.

Just a Parable

God and Satan were sitting at a table,
having a glass of wine just before
the beginning of everything.
Satan, a certifiable devil's advocate,
said, "Look, it's a spectacular idea,
but you as the very God you say you are
should know it doesn't stand a chance in hell
of actually working out."
God sighed - the desert winds were born -
smiled a smile
more infinitely mysterious than Mona Lisa's,
and finally said
"Ok, then, do you worst, you will anyway.
You won't - you can't -
realize that your cosmic lack of understanding
is part of the unfolding of this whole living story
that will create and transform universes;
that even you, dear Dark One,
will be taken up into and transformed,
your burning, Lucifer,
become shining."
Satan felt a spring of water rise
from the depths of his being
into his eyes,
but he rose and pushed the table over,
shattered his wine glass
on the mist that was
already turning into sacred boulders,
and stormed off cursing,
already plotting what he would do;
trying to blockade
the infinitely mysterious aching in his heart.

Kerstin Berger (model/makeup artist)
Hermann Berger (photographer)

Maya

Susan Daubenspeck

Susan Daubenspeck worked many years as an oncology nurse.

Intruder

We were standing in my kitchen. My left arm was duct taped
To my side around my waist. He positioned my right hand on
The cutting board moving my other fingers and lightly tapping
Them away from my middle finger. My F-you finger, I thought.
He didn't say anything or look at me so intent he was to get my
Hand just as he wanted. As he leaned over me I saw how precise
The part was in his hair. As if chiseled.
Then he took my largest knife out of the black knife block and
He held it up in the air. I remember hearing the living room clock
Click to another second. That knife down hard onto the cutting board
As he neatly severed my finger.
I heard myself scream but also heard a calm voice inside me
Telling me, "Right now was the time to act". That I must grab
The knife he had just dropped onto the counter. And with
Everything in me pick it up and plunge it hard and deep into
His pimpled neck.
And so I did - with a strength and ease that surprised me. He
Staggered a little and started to bleed out like a full open hose.
He fell to the kitchen floor. I thought of stabbing him in the heart.
But by the look in his eyes I could see there was no need. Still,
I stood over him for what seemed hours, probably five minutes.
With another knife I managed to cut the tape from my left arm.
Then I grabbed a kitchen towel and held it tight to my hand.
I picked up my finger and put it in a bowl with ice.
He hadn't moved. His eyes were glassy marbles. So I ran into
My room and grabbed my phone from its charger. I ran back to
The kitchen to make sure he was still dead. He was. And then
I dialed 9-1-1.
Now I look up at the detective standing over my hospital bed.
And I see wetness in her eyes. And maybe something else in her
Face. I think she is proud of me. Like she's thinking,' the old
Lady got the bad guy'. I know that I'll go free and not be judged
In a court of law. I will judge myself though, over and over, wondering.
I look down the hospital hallway after the detective leaves. The world
Is not better than before, nor is it worse. It is, however, definitely different.

Tito Perez

Tito Perez was born in the middle of the South Texas cotton fields. He worked over thirty years as an educator. He wrote grants and proposals. He was a speech writer, and taught grantsmanship. He is a spoken word artist, and poet. He has customized license plates for his car and truck.

Tito Perez

"Ondas (Insights) have been coming to me for years and I have been jotting them down all along. I believe Ondas will cease coming to me only when I die. In the meantime, I'll keep writing Ondas and sharing them with the world. This is my mission in life."

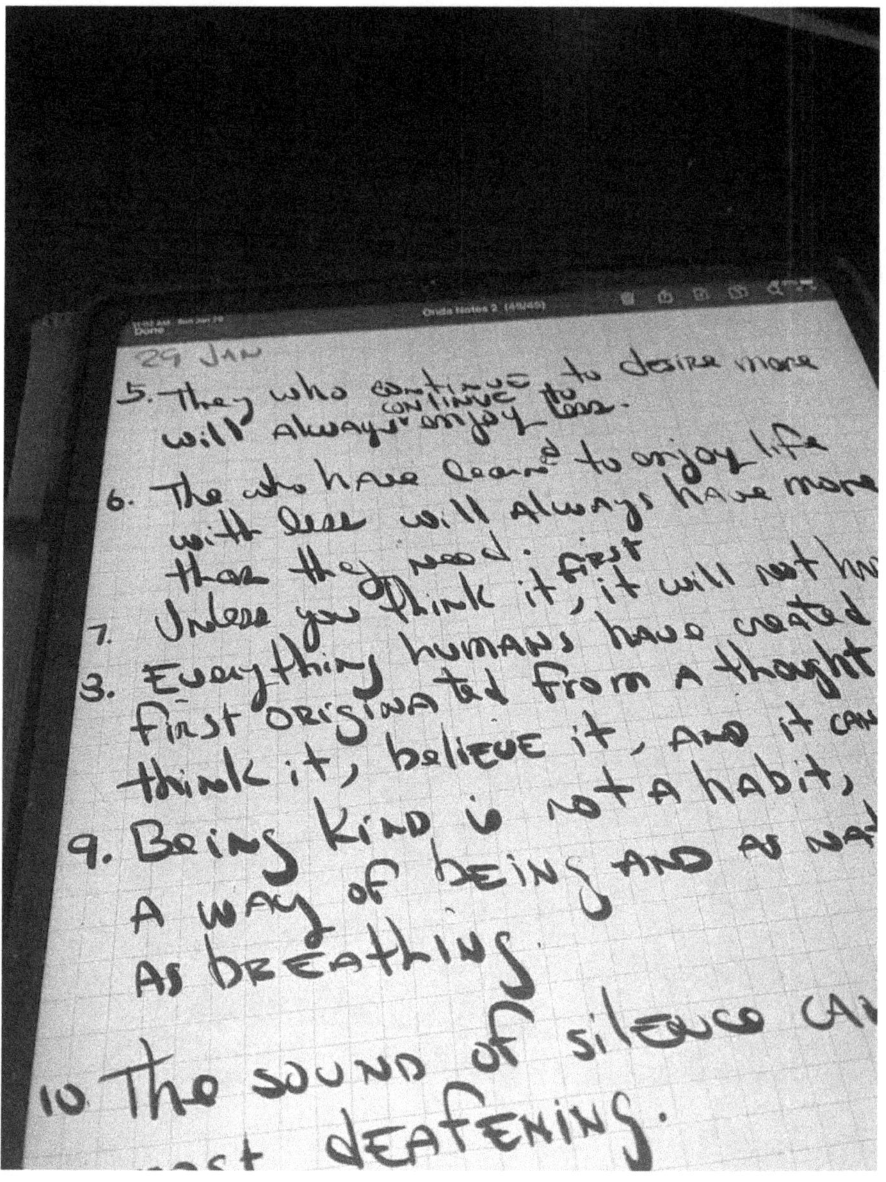

Tito Perez

"Journaling can be both meditative and therapeutic. When you put your thoughts and feelings on paper you acknowledge your reality while reflecting on your aspirations and your concerns. Journal and stay in touch with yourself."

Tom Murphy

Tom Murphy was the 2021-2022 Corpus Christi Poet Laureate and the *Langdon Review*'s 2022 Writer-In-Residence. Murphy has written several books and he's been widely published in literary journals and anthologies.

Palm frond shadows sway

Palm frond shadows sway

Typhus in my veins pills to kill

the virus that itches all over my body.

It didn't help when they shaved

my chest, besides ripping the hair

out every new time to put on an

EKG. I get messages: we prayed,

we care, we're wondering if you can

give us your voice, give us your

approval—let people know you are

with us, whether you are or not.

I'm the shadows of the fronds dancing.

Cannot be captured, cannot be changed

to do anything else except dance

until I fall to the ground and die.

Tongue cut off

Tongue cut off
grew again
speaking
off the cuff

Honky discourse
all I've unknown
conduct myself
as other

other than my sex
other than my skin
other reclaimed
outsider

I'm Thomas
or Tom
from my grandfather
Tom Green

Who died
at fifty-four,
four years
before I was born.

Kids laugh at what is awkward
not knowing or understanding
laugh out their
lack of knowledge

curiosity helps free you
from xenophobia
laugh and learn, child
learn and love

Ah, Cosy

Ah, Cosy,
          The stones we touched.
I imagine you now leaner, tramping
best maps take you into war zones
hefting an RPG through building rubble
fighting for water and warmth in Ukraine.

Remember rolling smokes on the outside table
of the Red Lion's beer garden in the middle
of the North Henge, the Sun Henge of Avebury?
Wadsworth 6X our mutual pints as we were wiled
in simpler times. Though you roll with gritty fingers
in the dark since Putin's strafing has snuffed out

light. Ah, Cosy, I'm afraid
to email you again, afraid to receive
your silent death in response. I'm afraid
our assent on Silbury, our walk through
the mound and around the Sarsens, mere pipe
dream before constant bombardment explodes.

Ah, Cosy, the world is full of hate
while others get rich and drink
their profits with babes' blood.
Things fall apart, but to expect
a deus ex machina; ludicrous.
The ungodly light blinds.

Tonāntzin Rodríguez

Tonāntzin Rodríguez is a mother, poet, curandera, activist, & photojournalist.

The Making of A Chingona

If you grew up without the protection of a father and were raised by two powerful women, Mi Madre y Mi Abuela, you knew a little chingona was in the making.

Leaving your country and loved ones behind y tener que cruzar el Rio Grande de chavalita. Night had fallen en el monte and we hid from La

Migra. Frightened, staring up at the heavens and luminous stars. The only protection was my mother's warm arms.

I didn't know the language and was a stuttering scared child in school. I had to work harder than most kids. Overcoming a speech impediment, earning good grades, and becoming fluent in both languages by the age of ten because I disliked how some folks ignored and discriminated against my non-English speaking mom who couldn't read or write. Our struggles have always been my motivation. I went to school for both of us. I was her secretary, helped fill out forms, and send payments. I also became her personal translator. Then she would volunteer me to translate for total strangers. At the schools, clinics, hospitals, washeterias, you name it. Not knowing then, she was already developing my public speaking skills. I was an active girl who liked the outdoors. Some called me a tomboy cause I preferred to play sports and could play better than some of the boys. Freshman year, I was picked up by varsity coach to be the point guard. That was a big chingona moment for me.

Then the boy problems began. You see, I've been blessed with many gifts. But most men only see the outer gifts. When they get to know me and don't get me, they will try to control me.

I gave seven years to the first husband. Love can make you act like a pendeja at times. You give him your bank card and allow him to drive your car. He was in and out of jail for unpaid tickets and couldn't hold down a job. When I bared my soul and told him about my battles with depression, he says to me, "so now I have have to pay for someone else's broken plates."

Within the first year of dating I was already going mad. And still, I married that mulato merenguero, sweet talking culero. Like I said, love can make you do some stupid shit. He was insecure and intimidated by my independence. Didn't understand my creative nature and told me I was too old to become a writer, at twenty-five. Worse was dealing with his passive aggressive techniques.

I began to die inside….I couldn't be me

Years kept passing by. I couldn't create art and I couldn't create a life. The baby he desperately wanted. I underwent many procedures and sobadas that would leave me in physical and emotional pain, but he wouldn't allow me to complain. When I said that I wanted to adopt. He said, "no, I'm not raising anyone else's child, tiene que ser di mi sangre." That would be the last time he'd break my heart. I always knew that I would be a mother and realized at that moment that it was not going to be by his side.

Y como dice Mi Jefa,
"se me va mucho a la chingada!"

That pelado had to go
and La Chingona returned!

She will not hide or be silenced again. And to those who beat her as child and as a young woman, you didn't get to brake this cabrones. You only made me stronger. Taught me how to take a stand and fight back. No man will ever lay a hand on me with anger. I can be a lamb or I can be a lion.

I will no longer be ashamed of who I am. I'm an artistic mujer. Proud to be a Mexicana. I will speak my language and wear my cultura with pride. Reclaiming my indigenous roots in this country which sits on sacred lands.

I will not be manipulated by society. Material things don't define me. I come from the world of souls and during my stay I will not be a slave to any government, money, or religious institution. Because a good Catholic woman doesn't get tattoos, drinks, smokes, and swears. And, I'm not supposed to practice yoga, meditation, or masturbation. C'mon! How am I supposed to elevate?

Not here to meet anyone's expectations. I chose to come to earth to fulfill Creator's goals. You can fly with me or let me be.

I don't like labels
But you
You can call me Chingona
I don't mind
I've earned it.

Wayne Hankins

Wayne Hankins lives in Corpus Christi, Texas. He studied creative writing, painting, architecture, and computer science; he worked for 25 years as a systems & software engineer in flight simulation trainers.

Silver Lined

It was the mischief
in her eyes.

You learned
she was smarter and funnier
than you
or anyone you'd known.

More creative, observant, tougher
than most - challenging, every day.

She led you - to art:
music, literature, painting, design.

Could stay awake through any night
and talk as long as you.

Passionate -
about everything that interested her.
Lucky you.

Every man met fell in love -
none harder.
Lucky you.

Didn't get a tenth of time wanted -
but made you more, better.
Lucky you.

Very.

William Mays

William Mays is the editor of the *Corpus Christi Writers* series. *George: The Lost Year* is the middle novel in his series *The Saga of George*. Listen to Mays read this excerpt on the MaysPublishing.com YouTube channel.

George: The Lost Year CHAPTER ONE

George took the last puff off the last joint and wondered when, or if, Uncle Nick would arrive. Three days had passed. Very Biblical. And way too long. It was only a two-day drive from Houston to Colorado. Something had gone wrong. There was only one explanation. Lazarus had killed Nick and, any second, he would break down the door to George's motel room and shoot him too.

The roach glowed a bright red as he puffed. Little more than an ember, it stuck to his thumb. He tried to shake it off, but it wouldn't come loose. Staying perfectly still despite the searing pain, he took careful aim with the nail of his middle finger and struck it full force. It shot forward, still burning, veered to the right, and landed in the garbage can overflowing with crumpled paper sacks and half-eaten carryout meals.

The last thing he needed was a fire. He would have checked on it, but squeaking wheels distracted him. They rolled down the cement breezeway outside his room, growing louder as they approached. It had to be Lazarus. He had come with so many guns that he needed a cart to carry them all, and they were so heavy that the wheels strained under the weight.

He got Original Sin from where he'd hidden it between the mattress and box springs and tiptoed to the peephole with his finger curled around the trigger.

It was only the maids with a cart full of towels and sheets.

A shower would calm his nerves and help him figure out what to do. He laid the gun on the bed and dropped his clothes on the floor. The warm, soapy-smelling steam enveloped him, and, like mighty Zeus, he drifted in the clouds in the celestial realms, joining Apollo, Athena, and, last but not least, Dionysus, the god of wine and revelry. There were some other Gods, but they didn't wear name tags. A pack of hippies crashed the party. They brought lots of dope to smoke. And Kelly materialized in the mist dressed in white robes. "I'm going to give you another chance," she said. "Don't fuck it up." Oh, he was glad to see her.

Feet marched down the breezeway, the sound vibrating through the thin wall. They were heavy, clunky men's feet in hard-soled shoes. They stopped at his door. Knuckles rapped on the wood.

He crept out of the shower dripping and naked, picked up Original Sin, and put his eye on the peephole. A swarthy man in khakis and a white t-shirt stood outside. He had to be Greek, but that didn't mean anything. There was a stain on his T-shirt, like tomato paste. That didn't mean anything, either. Lazarus could have sent an assassin who worked as a cook when he wasn't killing people. Life was an ongoing existential crisis. An enemy would look exactly like a friend. You never knew the truth until later, and then it didn't matter.

Nick stepped up next to the man. In an uncertain universe, there was one constant: family. They would never betray him. George slid Original Sin back under the mattress, put on his jeans, and unlocked the door. Like a soldier on a dangerous mission, Nick stepped inside and surveyed the unmade bed and the clothes and trash on the floor. "You remember Minas, don't you?" he said in Greek, the Marlboro in his mouth bobbing up and down as he talked. "He works here in Durango at The Golden Flame. You met him at the wedding when we met Maria's family."

George had only been fourteen at the time of that wedding, so he didn't remember him, but Minas would be insulted if he said he didn't. "Oh, yes, of course."

They hugged like best friends.

Nick sniffed the air. "Something's on fire."

George smelled it too. It wasn't the sweet fragrance of marijuana. It was a harsh, acrid odor.

A plume of smoke rose from the trash.

The roach had set the leftovers on fire!

William Walton

William Walton grew up on a ranch in the Texas Hill Country. He graduated from Bandera High School, and then Yale University. His collected fiction is available in *Madmen and Fellow Travelers*.

Rough Men, Smooth Hands

Casey knew he had no business going into the Rumble Inn when he saw a couple dozen motorcycles, but no cars, in the parking lot. But, shirt plastered to his sweaty back, he badly needed a cold one, and it was the only bar in town.

When he entered, the smell of stale beer, cigarettes, and urine overpowered him. He knew the stink would remain in his clothes long after he left. He wiped the sweat from his forehead with his shirt sleeve.

Yeah, coming in here was not such a good idea.

Relief from the oppressive heat of the outdoors was immediate, but it took a few minutes for his eyes to adjust to the darkened interior. Except for the backlit bar, the only light came from a jukebox and fluorescent beer signs scattered about the walls. A Willie Nelson song could be heard above the low murmur of voices.

Casey noted that most of the men wore T-shirts and black leather vests bearing the insignia of the Assassins, a notorious regional biker gang. The few women were equally divided between biker babes and locals, with maybe a couple of whores mixed in.

As he made his way through the crowded dance floor toward the bar, he accidentally brushed one of the patrons.

The biker glared at Casey. "Hey, watch where you're going, asshole."

"Sorry," Casey replied and kept walking.

"You're lucky I don't kick your butt."

Casey ignored the remark and made his way to the one empty stool at the bar. "Hey, barkeep, I'd like a beer. Make it a Shiner bock."

"Hold your horses. I'll get to you when it's your turn."

"Well, *pardon* me."

After a few minutes, the bartender brought Casey his beer.

He took a few gulps while checking out his surroundings.

The man seated to Casey's right had a sweat-stained cap, dirty T-shirt, and scruffy beard, but what captured Casey's attention were his hands. They were soft and smooth, with an almost manicured look. Casey couldn't take his eyes off them.

A burly biker tapped Casey on the shoulder. "I want this stool, so move your ass."

"Why don't you just wait until a spot opens up?" Casey replied.

"You wait for a spot. I'm taking yours."

Casey put his beer down on the bar. "I don't like being treated like a stool sample."

"I don't care what you like. Move it! Now!"

The man seated to Casey's right turned and faced the aggressive biker. "Wait for a spot, Turk. Leave this guy alone."

"Big Boy, I didn't know it was you. No offense, man. I'd never mistreat a friend of yours."

"He's not a friend of mine, but you'll leave him alone anyway."

"Whatever you say, Big Boy." Turk turned back to Casey. "Sorry, fella." He moved quickly away from the bar.

Big Boy turned and looked at Casey. "So, now tell me what the fuck you've been staring at?"

"I was just noticing your hands, how smooth they are. You're obviously not a man who does a lot of manual labor."

"No, I don't do any. You might say I'm in management."

Casey looked at the skull on Big Boy's dirty T-shirt. "What do you manage?"

"I'm head of this biker gang, the Assassins."

"That must be interesting."

"Hey, it's just like running any other business."

"What does your business consist of?" Casey asked.

"It's mostly collections, although I also distribute some weed and run a few prostitutes. Collections are my bread and butter."

Casey smiled. "What do you collect, butterflies?"

The biker did not return his smile. "Do I look like a butterfly sort of guy?"

"No." Casey's expression became more serious. "So, what do you collect?

"Debts that other businesses are unable to. They pay me a percentage to do the collecting for them."

"What if someone can't pay you?"

"I usually give them more time. Most ultimately pay me."

"But what if they don't or can't?"

"Then I cut off one of their fingers and give them more time to come up with the money. If they don't pay me when the time is up, I'll cut off another."

"So if I couldn't pay what I owed you, you'd cut off one of my fingers?"

"Yes, but please understand that it is only as a last resort. I very rarely have do that."

A prostitute approached Casey. "Hey baby, let's you and me go get it on."

Before Casey could reply, Big Boy intervened. "Millie, get lost. I'm having a conversation with this guy." Millie quickly moved away.

"Is that prostitute one of yours?" Casey watched Millie cross the room.

"You mean that crack whore?"

"Is there any other kind?" Casey laughed. "Oh, you mean the drug."

"Hey, you're a smart ass. I like that. I'm Big Boy Baker." He extended his hand.

Casey shook it. "I'm Casey Dawson," he said.

"Casey, you know you have no damned business in here, don't you? What do you think Turk would have done if I hadn't jumped in?"

"Yeah, I was hot and thirsty, but it was pretty stupid of me. Do you think I ought to haul ass?"

"No. You are under my protection now, so you have nothing to fear."

"But, I expect I ought not come in here again. Right?"

"Come in any time you want. I'll put the word out you're not to be messed with. However, it would be a good idea for you to avoid other places like this. No point asking for trouble."

"Big Boy, when you were talking about your business weren't you at all concerned that I might be a cop?"

"Hell no. I can smell a cop a mile away. No way you're one."

"Well, I am and you are under arrest," Casey said. "Put your hands behind your back."

"You're shitting me!" Big Boy's eyes got wide.

"Of course I am. I'm just playing around." Casey smiled.

Big Boy's voice was ice cold. "Sometimes comedians think they are so funny they don't notice when no one laughs."

He pulled out a switchblade, flipped it open, and shaved some hair off his forearm to demonstrate its sharpness. Casey forgot all about Big Boy's smooth hands. His smile disappeared.

Big Boy laid the flat side of the blade on the back of Casey's hand, which was resting on the bar. "I'll only take one of your little fingers because yours is a minor offense."

Casey withdrew his hand. "Surely you don't mean that. I was just making a joke."

"I didn't find it funny."

"I'm sorry. Please don't cut me."

"Nah, I won't. I'm just messing with you."

"Crap, you really had me going there."

"You're pretty ballsy for a college boy type. You sure you don't want to learn to be a biker?

"I don't think I'm cut out for that."

"No, I don't expect you are," Big Boy said. "Buy you a beer?"

Sarah K. Lenz

Photo/Commentary

Why should visual artists have all the fun with switching mediums? I love how my words flow differently when I type on a manual machine. On typewriters, I tap into a creative zone that I don't find on computer or in longhand.